THEMATIC UNIT

THANKSGIVING

Written By Ireta Sitts Graube

Illustrated by Sue Fullam

Teacher Created Materials, Inc.
6421 Industry Way
Westminster, CA 92683
www.teachercreated.com
©*1992 Teacher Created Materials, Inc.*
Reprinted, 2001
Made in U.S.A.
ISBN-1-55734-258-X

Table of Contents

Introduction

Thanksgiving contains a captivating whole language, thematic unit. Its 80 exciting pages are filled with a wide variety of lesson ideas and activities designed for use with primary children. At its core are three 18 high-quality children's literature selections, *A Turkey for Thanksgiving, Silly Tilly's Thanksgiving Dinner,* and *Thanksgiving at the Tappletons'*. For each of these books, activities are included which set the stage for reading, encourage the enjoyment of the book, and extend the concepts gained. In addition, the theme is connected to the curriculum with activities in language arts, (including daily writing suggestions), math, science (design technology), social studies, art, music, and life skills (cooking). Many of these activities to encourage cooperative learning.

Suggestions and patterns for games and ideas for bulletin boards are additional time savers for the busy teacher. Furthermore, directions for teaching children about immigration and ancestors combined in an culminating activity, allow the students to synthesize their knowledge in order to produce products that can be shared beyond the classroom. All of these activities combine to make this book a very complete teacher resource.

This thematic unit includes:

❏ **literature selections**—summaries of three children's books with related lessons (complete with reproducible pages) that cross the curriculum

❏ **poetry**—suggested selections and lessons enabling students to write and publish their own works

❏ **planning guides**—suggestions for sequencing lessons each day of the unit

❏ **writing ideas**—daily suggestions as well as writing activities across the curriculum, including Big Books

❏ **bulletin board ideas**—suggestions and plans for student-created and/or interactive bulletin boards

❏ **homework suggestions**—extending the unit to the child's home

❏ **curriculum connections**—in language arts, math, science, social studies, art, music, and life skills such as cooking and physical education

❏ **group projects**—to foster cooperative learning

❏ **a culminating activity**—which requires students to synthesize their learning to produce a product or engage in an activity that can be shared with others

❏ **a bibliography**—suggesting additional literature and nonfiction books on the theme.

To keep this valuable resource intact so that it can be used year after year, you may wish to punch holes in the pages and store them in a three-ring binder.

Introduction (cont.)

Why Whole Language?

A whole language approach involves children in using all modes of communication: reading, writing, listening, observing, illustrating, experiencing, and doing. Communication skills are interconnected and integrated into lessons that emphasize the whole of language rather than isolating its parts. The lessons revolve around selected literature. Reading is not taught as a separate subject from writing and spelling, for example. A child reads, writes (spelling appropriately for his/her level), speaks, listens, etc. in response to a literature experience introduced by the teacher. In this way, language skills grow naturally, stimulated by involvement and interest in the topic at hand.

Why Thematic Planning?

One very useful tool for implementing an integrated whole language program is thematic planning. By choosing a theme with correlating literature selections for a unit of study, a teacher can plan activities throughout the day that lead to a cohesive, in-depth study of the topic. Students will be practicing and applying their skills in meaningful context. Consequently, they will tend to learn and retain more. Both teachers and students will be freed from a day that is broken into unrelated segments of isolated drill and practice.

Why Cooperative Learning?

Besides academic skills and content, students need to learn social skills. No longer can this area of development be taken for granted. Students must learn to work cooperatively in groups in order to function well in modern society. Group activities should be a regular part of school life, and teachers should consciously include social objectives as well as academic objectives in the planning. For example, a group working together to write a report may need to select a leader. The teacher should make the objectives clear to the students and monitor the qualities of good leader-follower group interaction just as he/she would state and monitor the academic goals of the project.

Why Big Books?

An excellent, cooperative, whole language activity is the production of Big Books. Groups of students or the whole class can apply their language skills, content knowledge, and creativity to produce a Big Book that can become a part of the classroom to be read and reread. These books make excellent culminating projects for sharing beyond the classroom with parents, librarians, and other classes. Big Books can be produced in many ways. This thematic unit book includes directions for one method you may choose.

Why Journals?

Each day your students should have the opportunity to write in a journal. They may respond to a book, write about a personal experience, or answer a general "question of the day" posed by the teacher. Students should be encouraged to refer to the posted vocabulary list to check their spelling. The cumulative journal provides an excellent means of documenting writing progress.

History of Thanksgiving

In the United States of America, Thanksgiving is celebrated on the fourth Thursday in November. In Canada, Thanksgiving is celebrated on the second Monday in October. Countries around the world set aside a day for giving thanks. Many of these holidays have much in common with harvest feasts that have been celebrated down through the centuries.

In biblical times there was a feast of the Tabernacles, or tents. Hebrew people lived in tents made of boughs and decorated them with leaves and branches. They feasted and thanked God for their harvest. Jewish people still celebrate this festival and call it Sukkot.

Ancient Greeks also had a harvest festival after their grain was cut in the fall. People visited the shrine of Demeter, the goddess of the harvest and put gifts of fruit, honey, and grain at her feet. They had a feast to celebrate her goodness.

The Romans held their harvest festival in October. Their goddess was Ceres and the festival was called the Cerelia. They believed Ceres guarded their crops and helped them grow. Our word "cereal" comes from the Greek word, Ceres. The people felt blessed with the crops Ceres had given them. They had parades, music, dancing, and played many kinds of games.

The Celtic people had a festival named Samhain, which they celebrated in early November. It was a combination harvest festival and a day of the dead. The Celtic people had a feast and gave offerings to their ancestors during this celebration.

Halloween celebrations can be traced to this ancient custom.

The English people had a festival they called Harvest Home. When the last wagon came in from the fields the whole village walked along beside the wagon singing songs and wearing flowers and ribbons. Sometimes feasts were held in barns.

History of Thanksgiving *(cont.)*

China has celebrated a Harvest Moon festival for many centuries. The moon is fullest on the fifteenth day of the eighth moon, or month, and this is when their celebration took place. We call this moon the harvest moon. The ancient farmers used the light so they could harvest more crops. Women baked round moon cakes and placed them on altars in the courtyards. At midnight, families celebrated with a moonlight feast.

Thanksgiving in Canada was probably started 53 years before the Pilgrims celebrated Thanksgiving in Massachusetts. English settlers under Sir Martin Frobisher held a harvest feast in Newfoundland. Today, Canadian families and friends share turkey, mashed potatoes, cranberry sauce, and pumpkin pie. Wild rice and maple syrup pie are two Canadian specialties that are often found on Canadian tables at Thanksgiving time.

American Pilgrims celebrated a special Thanksgiving day on July 30, 1623, in thanks for rain which had nourished their crops. After this there were other Thanksgiving festivals, though not one every year.

The native American bird, the turkey, became the center of the feast. They were not the fat gobblers we have today. They were freshly shot wild turkeys, much skinnier, with stringier and less juicy meat. The Pilgrims also ate goose, venison, partridge, and even an occasional beaver tail along with their turkey or in place of it.

Pumpkin and other members of the squash family were new to the Pilgrims. They did not grow in Europe. The Pilgrims were happy to learn about these plants from the Native Americans and made a beer out of pumpkins, parsnips, and walnut tree chips when their barley crops failed to prosper!

Corn was also new to the Pilgrims. With the Native Americans' help, the Pilgrims learned how to grow corn successfully. They were delighted to be able to dry it and pound it into flour for corn bread and corn meal mush.

Apples were gathered from the new trees brought over from England. Biscuits of coarse wheat flour were also served. Salads were made of watercress and leeks. Gooseberries and dried plums and cherries were also presented at this feast.

In 1863 President Abraham Lincoln proclaimed Thanksgiving a national holiday and set the date that we celebrate today.

A Turkey for Thanksgiving
by Eve Bunting
Summary

Mr. and Mrs. Moose are setting the table for Thanksgiving dinner. Mrs. Moose wishes she could have a turkey for dinner like everyone else. Hearing this, Mr. Moose sets out to find a turkey for his wife. As he searches, he finds his friends, Rabbit, Mr. and Mrs. Goat, Sheep, and Porcupine. They all tag along to help. Together they discover Turkey hiding in tall grass, not at all willing to be part of their Thanksgiving dinner. The delightful ending to this story will capture children's hearts.

The outline below is a suggested plan for using the various activities that are presented in this unit. You should adapt these ideas to fit your own classroom situation.

Sample Plan

Day 1

- Discuss the history of Thanksgiving and of wild turkeys. (pages 5-6)
- Make predictions about the book based on the picture on the cover. Record these on chart paper.
- Read A Turkey for Thanksgiving.
- Journal Writing (page 9) "How would you feel if you were a turkey?"
- Begin "I am thankful for . . ." collage. (page 10)
- Send home the turkey soup letter. (page 64)
- Send home Turkey Family art. (pages 55-57)

Day 2

- Continue making the collage. (page 10)
- Collage Writing lists. (page 10)
- Review the book. Reread the predictions made on Day 1. Discuss.
- Share the Journal Writing done on Day 1.
- Go on The Turkey Hunt. (page 12)
- Do the Language Activities with the pocket chart. (page 13)
- Write about the Turkey Hunt. (page 14)
- Do Story Math Problems. (page 15)
- Teach the song "Hickory, Dickory, Lurkey." (page 63)

Day 3

- Design a Turkey Hunt Story Map. (page 14)
- Do Turkey Egg Estimation. (page 16)

- Do Collage Math. (page 11)
- Make a Collage Science graph. (page 11)
- Grow sprouts for turkeys to eat. (page 50)
- Make bean sprout pictures. (page 50)
- Write about bean sprout pictures. (page 50)
- Introduce Design Technology with peas & toothpicks. (page 19)

Day 4

- Do a pre-design for Design Technology. (page 19)
- Build the pea & toothpick design. (page 19)
- Do a post-design and written description. (page 19)
- Follow the Turkey Trail. (page 44)
- Complete Turkey Hand Math. (page 48)
- Try Turkey Feather Writing. (page 42)

Day 5

- Play Turkey Berry, Gobble, Wobble. (page 20)
- Do Turkey Berry Writing. (page 21)
- Make Turkey Headpieces. (page 58)
- Learn turkey poem. (page 58)
- Wearing turkey headpieces, act out the poem.
- Make Turkey Soup. (page 64)
- Do Turkey Soup Math with cards. (page 65)

Overview of Activities

Setting the Stage

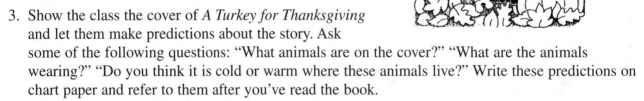

1. Prepare your classroom for this unit on Thanksgiving. Set up learning centers and displays with Thanksgiving items, feathers, and turkey books.

2. Make copies of the Family Turkey on pages 56 and 57. These copies may be enlarged and traced on construction paper or copied on 11" x 18" paper. Send the turkey home with the letter on page 55.

3. Show the class the cover of *A Turkey for Thanksgiving* and let them make predictions about the story. Ask some of the following questions: "What animals are on the cover?" "What are the animals wearing?" "Do you think it is cold or warm where these animals live?" Write these predictions on chart paper and refer to them after you've read the book.

4. Let the children help create a Thanksgiving collage bulletin board. Use it to complete several of the Thanksgiving collage activities on pages 10 and 11.

Enjoying the Book

1. Read *A Turkey for Thanksgiving* aloud to the whole class. Stop on page 23 and ask what they think will happen next. Compare these predictions to those they made after seeing only the cover of the book.

2. Finish reading the book. Discuss. Look at the predictions again.

3. Review the events in the story. What animal did Mr. Moose find first when he was looking for turkey? second? etc.

8

Overview of Activities *(cont.)*

Enjoying the Book *(cont.)*

---

4. Act out the story, letting eight children be the various animals. Other children can pretend to be chairs, table, food, etc., in the Moose household.

5. Make journals with the class. These can be constructed simply by stapling together several sheets of paper with a blank cover. Let children decorate their covers and write their names. They may write in their journals or draw pictures.

6. Go on a Turkey Hunt. Use the language extension activities on page 13. Write about the Turkey Hunt. Design a Turkey Hunt Story Map showing all the places you went and what you found.(page 14)

7. Do the Turkey Hunt Egg Estimation activity (page 16). Describe real turkey eggs, which are twice as large as ordinary chicken eggs. They are a pale, creamy-tan color, speckled with brown. If possible, use speckled jelly beans as a manipulative to complete this activity.

8. Read other books about turkeys and feathers. (See Bibliography on page 80 for suggestions.) Show pictures of wild turkeys and discuss.

9. Sing some songs about Thanksgiving. See page 63 for a song to go along with *A Turkey for Thanksgiving*.

Extending the Book

---

1. Encourage parents to read to children and children to read to parents. Have story bags available for overnight checkout. Make or purchase cloth bags and fill them with one stuffed animal and a book about that animal. For example, a bag with a stuffed or paper bag turkey would contain a book about turkeys or related Thanksgiving story. A bag with a stuffed bear could contain books about bears.

2. Get children thinking and problem solving. Introduce design technology with peas and toothpicks. As a class, do a predesign for your structure. Build the design out of peas and toothpicks. Draw a post-design and make a written description of how you built it (page 19). Once you have built one as a class, give students the opportunity to complete one on their own.

3. Remember back to what was on the Thanksgiving table at the Moose home. Mrs. Moose served Turkey some sprouts. Try growing sprouts and eating them (page 50).

4. Look at the culminating activities on pages 71-76. Begin to get students ready for these activities by talking to them about immigrants and how they came to North America. Let them start to think about all the different types of people that there are to share Thanksgiving with. Compare it to the Moose's dinner guests. The culminating activity would be appropriate to do now or when you have finished all three books.

Thanksgiving Collage Activities

Bulletin Board

Materials:

magazines, large piece of black or white butcher paper, construction paper, crayons, glue, scissors, bulletin board space

Teacher Directions:

Place a large piece of butcher paper on a bulletin board that the children can reach. Talk about all the things we are thankful for at Thanksgiving. Explain that a collage is a collection of pictures, drawings, scraps of paper, or items that can be glued or fastened to the paper. This Thanksgiving collage should help us remember all the reasons why we are thankful and happy.

Directions:

The children will cut out of magazines or draw and color items for which they are thankful. They can also bring pictures and items from home. They can use glue or fasten with pins the pictures or items that they bring. They may want to overlap edges and place together those things that have complementary colors.

Collage Writing

Have the children write down all the items they have put on the bulletin board to create their collage. From this list, make sentences telling why you are thankful for these items or people. Post these papers on the bulletin board near the collage or make a class book. This can easily be adapted into a Big Book by letting students choose one item from their collage list. Have them dictate or write a description onto a large sheet of paper and illustrate. Collect all the pages into a class Big Book. Title the book "Our Class Collage" and let children illustrate the cover. Have the class book available for home checkout.

Collage Activities *(cont.)*

Collage Math

1. Count and number all the items on the collage. Numbers can be written directly on the collage or written on small cards and taped beside the item with masking tape.

2. Count the items by 1's, 2's, 5's, or 10's.

3. Count all the people, animals, tools, furniture, etc. Make a graph showing the names and numbers of the various items. Give children a sticky note with the name of the item such as dog, car, dad. Let them stick it in the correct column: people, animals, or things. Then count the number of notes in each column.

people	animals	things
Dad	cat	soccer
Grandma	hippo	skates

Collage Science

Use the collage to complete the following activities. Ask the questions, "Which of these items are alive?" "Which are not alive?" Make a chart showing the items.

"Which of these items could you grow?" "Which are made from wood?" "Which items are made from plastics?" Make a list.

These items are made from wood.

1. chair
2. table
3. tree
4. swing
5. bowl

These items are made of plastic.

1. toy car
2. toy doll
3. chair
4. dishes
5. computer

Variations:

Have each child make his/her own collage on a smaller piece of butcher paper or large piece of construction paper. Or make all collages on 9" x 11" construction paper and organize into a class book with written explanations..

The Turkey Hunt

Have the children repeat a clapping, slapping rhythm with you. Clap your hands and then slap your knees. Ask the children to keep the rhythm going while you tell the story. Chant the following story to the rhythm:

"I'm going on a turkey hunt, a turkey hunt, a turkey hunt.

I'm going to find a turkey for Thanksgiving dinner.

I'm going to climb a tree and look around.

 (Keep the same rhythm, but pretend to climb a tree with hands. Next, look around with hand above eyes keeping the same rhythm.)

No turkey. (Clap, slap again.)

Down the tree I go. (Make hand motions to represent climbing down a tree.)

 (Begin clap, slap rhythm again with hands.)

Going to hike across this field. (Swishing motion with hands.)

No turkey. What's that?

A little lake. No bridge. I'll have to swim across it.

 (Make swimming motion with arms to the rhythm.)

Climb out. (Make climbing motion with hands.

I'm wet. (Shake body to rhythm.)

 (Resume clap, slap rhythm.)

What's that straight ahead? A big hill. I'll have to climb it.

 (Clap, slap rhythm slows down as he nears the top of hill and breathing is loud and slow.)

Up at last.

What's that over there going in the woods?

 (Look around with hand above eyes.)

 (Resume clap, slap rhythm.)

It looks like a wild turkey. It is a WILD TURKEY! Let's go catch him. Down the hill fast.

 (Speed up clap, slap rhythm.)

'Hey, Turkey! Do you want to come home with me for Thanksgiving dinner?'

 (Resume regular clap, slap rhythm.)

'NO WAY!' yelled the turkey and he flew into the woods.

 (Slow clapping, slapping down.)

Guess we'll have to eat chicken this year!"

Variations:

1. Vary the game by asking the children where they want to go and follow their suggestions as you go on the hunt.

2. Have the children tell what else they found in addition to the turkey for Thanksgiving dinner, i.e. "I found a turkey and a sweet potato." Keep the rhythm going as they each tell what they will take to Thanksgiving dinner. If you want to strengthen listening and memory skills, have them repeat what the person before them said, and then name their own item.

The Turkey Hunt (cont.)

Language Activities

Reproduce these word cards onto index or heavy paper. Cut them out. Have the children place these cards in the correct Turkey Hunt sequence in a pocket chart or on the floor. Then use the pictures on page 17 and have the children match the pictures to the word cards.

Turkey Hunt
tree
lake
hill
wood
turkey

The Turkey Hunt (cont.)

Writing Activities

Choose some of these writing activities.

1. List all the places that we went to look for a turkey. Put them the correct story order; i.e. 1) tree 2) field 3) lake.

2. Tell what you would bring to Thanksgiving dinner in place of the turkey.

3. How would you catch the turkey?

4. Describe how the turkey looks. What color is he? How big is he?

5. Write a Turkey Hunt story of your own. Where would you go? What would you see?

6. Use the picture cards on page 17. Let children write stories about them.

Story Map

Using paper, crayons, or colored pencils or pens, make a story map of The Turkey Hunt. Think about all the places the characters went to look for a turkey. Where on the page do you want your story to start? Do you want the beginning of your story in the upper left hand corner, lower right, etc.? Show the trail that the turkey hunter followed while looking for the turkey.

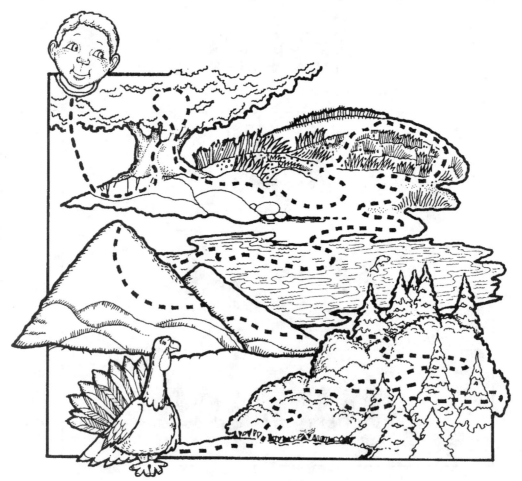

14

The Turkey Hunt *(cont.)*

Story Math Problems

Materials:

white or speckled jellybeans or beans or counters, 9" x 11" brown construction paper, crayons, pencils and writing paper

Directions:

Let students solve the problems with beans. Have them write the problem down on writing paper after they have used the beans. Tell the following story problems to the class.

"You found the turkey, but he started to run off very fast. You were able to follow him very quietly. He didn't know you were behind him and he went straight to his nest. Mother Turkey was there setting on their eggs. They had four eggs in the nest. " (Have the children draw a circle with a crayon on the brown construction paper and place 4 eggs in it.) *"You decided to take one egg for Thanksgiving dinner. How many were left?"* Have them tell you or write down the equation on paper. Continue this type of problem solving with the children.

For more advanced math, bring in more turkeys and more nests. For example: *"If every child in this room found one turkey and one egg, how many turkeys and eggs would we have altogether?"* or *"If every boy in the room found one turkey and two eggs, how many turkeys and eggs altogether?"*

The Turkey Hunt *(cont.)*

Turkey Egg Estimation

Materials:

white or speckled jelly beans, clear jar, large piece of paper and pen or chalkboard, tens board, small 6" containers or cups

Teacher Preparation:

Materials: 11" x 18" white construction paper, 9" x 11" blue construction paper, glue, black marker

Directions: Make a tens board out of an 11" x 18" piece of white construction paper. Paste a 9" x 11" piece of blue construction paper on one side. Mark 10 "X's" on the blue side.

White (tens)	Blue (ones)
	X X X X X X X X X X

Directions:

How many "turkey eggs" do you think are in this jar? Write the estimations down on the paper or the chalkboard. When everyone has had a turn, count the "eggs" using the tens board. Place each egg on an "X" on the one's side of the board. When you have a set of ten, place the set in a cup and move it to the 10's side of the board (the white side). When you have more than one set of ten, count by tens every cup on the tens side. When the final count is made, look at the estimations and have the children tell you which number is the closet estimation. Ask whether each number is more than or less than the correct number of eggs.

Extension:

Have two sets of number cards from 0-9 (page 18) and let the children place them in front of each side of the tens board after you have finished counting the "eggs." The board and the numbers should "face" the children.

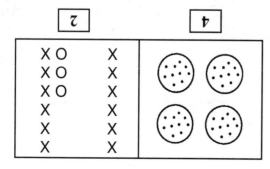

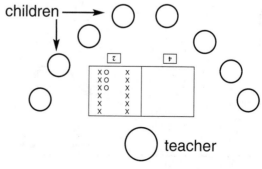

The Turkey Hunt (cont.)

Picture Cards

Use these picture cards to complete The Turkey Hunt activities on page 13 and 14.

The Turkey Hunt *(cont.)*

Number Cards

Use these number cards to complete The Turkey Hunt activities on page 16.

0	**1**
2	**3**
4	**5**
6	**7**
8	**9**

Design Technology

Do you think Mr. and Mrs. Moose served peas to their guests at Thanksgiving? Did you know you could build with peas, rather than eat them?

Materials:

pea seeds (purchase packages in garden shops), colored or plain round toothpicks, large bowl, water, small containers, 2" x ¼" strips of construction paper, small paper circles, glue

Teacher Preparation:

Soak the dried peas overnight. Just before you plan to use the peas, drain them and place them in small containers. Demonstrate how to use peas as joints and toothpicks as building blocks.

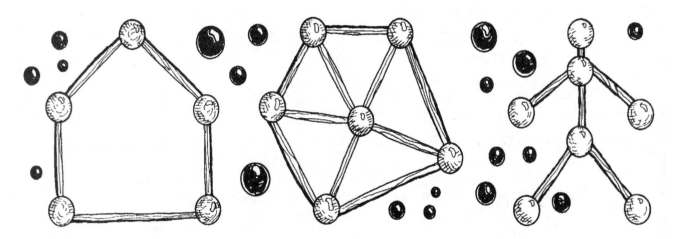

Directions:

Use the toothpicks as the building blocks and the softened peas as joints. The children will soon discover that they can build geometric designs, people, toys, animals, etc.

When they have completed their design or figure, let them dry for one to two days. The peas will shrink up and the toothpicks will be firmly jointed to the structures.

After the children have had a first experience with building pea structures, let them do a pre-design on paper before building another structure. This requires planning and problem solving before they start building. These pictures can be drawn with pencils, colored pencils, or crayons. Or the children can use 2" x ¼" strips of construction paper to represent the toothpicks and small paper circles to represent the peas. They can "build" their pre-design with these paper representations.

Following their pre-design, they will build the structure with peas and toothpicks. If they find they can not follow the design, they will need to change the structure. After their project is completed, have them draw a post design. Did it turn out exactly as planned? If so, why did it work and if not, why not?

Have the students describe in their writing journal exactly how they made their structure. Have them give it to another child and see if the child can build the structure following the written directions.

Turkey Berry, Gobble, Wobble

Play this game to enhance visual recognition. Then do some follow-up, using some activities on page 21.

Materials:

One small turkey, a plastic fruit or vegetable, or any small item related to the Thanksgiving theme

Directions: This game is similar to "Hide the Thimble." Show the children the object which will be hidden. Hide the object in an obvious spot in the room where children do not have to open anything or look inside anything to find it.

When a child sees the item he/she walks away without acknowledging it and says "Turkey Berry, Gobble, Wobble." This alerts everyone that he/she has seen the item, but does not tell the other children who are looking for it where it is located. All children continue looking for the item until everyone has seen it. The child who finds the item last will be the next person to hide the object. Or, let a person who didn't give away it's hiding place hide the object next.

As a variation, name the game after the item you are hiding. For instance, "Apple, Bapple," if you are hiding a small apple.

Extensions:

1. Use directions to cue the children, i.e. "The object is hidden in the southwest corner of the room." These directions can be given orally or written on the chalkboard. For younger children, give clues such as, "Look up" or "Look down."

2. Hide words, letter cards, numbers or anything you are trying to teach in the classroom.

Turkey Berry, Gobble, Wobble *(cont.)*

Writing

Writing Ideas:

1. Describe where you will put the object when it is your turn to hide it.
2. Make a list of all the places in the room where the object could be hidden.
3. Describe what you did when you saw the object. How did you act? Where did you go? Did anyone else see you? Were you the first person to see it?
4. Pretend you are the object and you are being hidden. How do you feel? Where is your favorite hiding spot in the room?
5. Describe the object that is being hidden.

Art

Materials:

11" x 18" drawing paper or construction paper, pencil, crayons or watercolors

Directions:

Display the object in a position where all children can easily see it. Discuss what the object looks like. Ask the children to describe it. What shape is it? Encourage the children to draw it bigger than the actual size. Draw the object. Color the object with crayons or watercolors.

Extension:

Display the pictures with the children's written description of the object or make a Big Book. Put together all the pages and illustrations onto large paper. Bind and add a title and cover. The children will enjoy seeing all the different pictures of the same object and the varying written descriptions.

Music

Let the children help make up a song to sing while they are waiting for all the children to find the object. Here is an example to the tune of
"Free Jacques" or "Are You Sleeping, Brother John?"

Can you find it?
Can you find it?
Where is it?
Where is it?
Somewhere in our classroom,
Somewhere in our classroom
I see it.
I see it.

Silly Tilly's Thanksgiving Dinner

by Lillian Hoban

Summary

Silly Tilly Mole drops and smudges her glasses and all her Thanksgiving plans turn into a haze and a fog. Where are the invitations? Where did she put her recipes? Why is everything in her world covered in fog?

Mr. Bunny accidentally comes to her rescue, giving this funny story a happy ending.

The outline below is a suggested plan for using the various activities that are presented in this unit. You should adapt these ideas to fit your own classroom situation.

Sample Plan

Day 1

- Discuss the animal on the cover of *Silly Tilly's Thanksgiving Dinner*. What kind of an animal is Silly Tilly?

- Read *Silly Tilly's Thanksgiving Dinner* to the class.

- Discuss the confusion with Silly Tilly. What happened to her glasses? Was she forgetful?

- Show a photograph of a mole. Discuss.

- Plan a Silly Tilly Fondue & Fruit Party. (page 28)

- Send home letter to parents. (page 29)

- Tell children to save and bring in feathers for later study.

- Plant corn seeds. (page 51)

- Sequence the corn planting. (page 52)

Day 2

- Reread and review the book.

- Write in journals: How do you think Turkey felt when he wasn't invited to dinner?

- Do corn estimating activity. (page 49)

- Play "Corn, Corn! Who Has the Corn?" (page 49)

- Sing "Here We Go Over to Silly Tilly's." (page 62)

Day 3

- Play Turkey Put Together. (pages 46-47)

- Ask children to bring in fruit; record on chart. (page 28)

- Copy fruit (page 30) and vegetable (page 66) cards. Let children color them. Laminate.

- Write Silly Tilly's Recipes. (page 68)

- Make Mr. Chipmunk's Cranberry Stew Relish. (page 68)

Day 4

- Play games with fruit and vegetable cards.

- Pop popcorn in class. (page 25)

- Discuss Mr. Turkey's popcorn; make a popcorn turkey. (page 25)

- Do Popcorn Writing. (page 26)

- Do Popcorn Drawing. (page 26)

- Play Cooperative Popcorn Math. (page 27)

Day 5

- Have the Fondue and Fruit Party. (page 29)

- Look at feathers with magnifying glass. Do feather science experiments. (page 53)

- Draw a feather. (page 54)

- Try feather writing. (page 42)

- Have a feather race. (page 54)

Overview of Activities

Setting the Stage

1. In addition to Thanksgiving books, collect books about moles, rabbits, squirrels, woodchucks, chipmunks, mice, and turkeys. Make these available in the library center.

2. Discuss past Thanksgiving dinners. What do children remember about them? What members of their family or friends did they eat with? What do they like about Thanksgiving?

3. Let children draw pictures of food they have eaten at Thanksgiving dinners in the past or cut pictures out of magazines and glue them on a 9" x 18" piece of construction paper.

4. Discuss moles. Look at books and pictures of real moles. Read *Molly in Danger*. See Bibliography (page 80) for more book suggestions. Show a picture of Silly Tilly from the book. Does she look like a mole? How is she the same? How does she differ?

5. Draw a mole. Show children the step-by-step method on the board and let them try to draw their own.

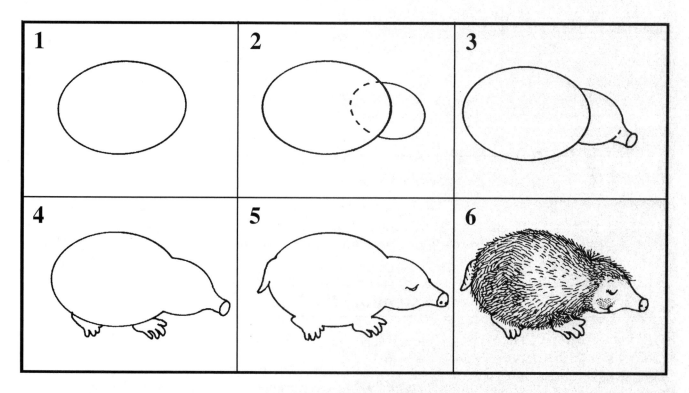

Enjoying the Book

1. Read *Silly Tilly's Thanksgiving Dinner* to the class. Discuss what happened and why it happened. What was wrong with Tilly?

2. Teach the song, "Here We Go Over To Silly Tilly's" to the class. Write the words on chart paper and post it in the classroom (page 62).

Overview of Activities (cont.)

Enjoying the Book (cont.)

3. List the other animals that are in the book, i.e. rabbit, squirrel, woodchuck, chipmunk, fieldmouse, and turkey. Beside each animal list its characteristics. The children might also want to list the name of the food that each animal brought to the dinner.

Animal	Characteristics	Food to Silly Tilly's
rabbit	long ears	sweet potato pie

4. Write recipes for pine nut cake, cranberry stew, or sweet potato pie. (page 68)

5. Compile all the recipes into a class book entitled "Silly Tilly's Thanksgiving Recipes." Next to each recipe the children can draw a picture of what the dish might look like. Add a Table of Contents telling where each child's recipe can be found in the book. Make this book available for overnight check out.

Extending the Book

1. Plan a Silly Tilly Fondue & Fruit Party. Send home letters on page 29 to request food and invite parents.

2. Play Fruit and Vegetable games on page 29. Make copies of pages 30 and 66 and let the children color the cards. Laminate the cards or cover with contact paper. Ask the children to find a partner and play "Concentration" with the fruit cards. Add the vegetable cards on page 66 and make the game more difficult. Use these cards for language games, spelling words, and writing lessons.

3. Start a science center with different varieties of feathers. Get books about feathers and birds. Provide magnifying glasses or a microscope for the children to examine the feathers in detail. Discuss the parts of a feather. Try writing with a feather quill dipped in ink or thin paint. See page 53 for more feather study.

Best Ever Popcorn Activities

Popcorn Turkey

Mr. Turkey brought corn to Silly Tilly's Dinner and made his recipe for Best Ever Popcorn. We can try to do the same.

Teacher Preparation:

With the class helping decide what is the best way to pop corn, choose from microwave, the top of the stove, or a corn popper. Write down the steps involved in making popcorn. Then pop the corn for this project. Make copies of the turkey neck pattern. Make enough patterns so every five children shares one pattern.

Materials:

unbuttered and unsalted popped popcorn, 9" x 11" white construction paper, small pieces or scraps of red and black construction paper, glue, scissors, crayons, tagboard for neck patterns

Directions:

Give each child a 9" x 11" white paper. Have them draw a large circle on it. Trace the neck pattern on one side of the circle. Place a small amount of glue on one part of the circle or neck and begin sticking on popcorn. Add a wattle using red construction paper and black construction paper for the eyes. Draw the feet and color them with a yellow or orange crayon.

Best Ever Popcorn Activities *(cont.)*

Popcorn Writing

Materials:

journals or writing paper, popcorn ready to eat (to avoid greasy papers, don't butter the popcorn), *The Popcorn Book* by Tomie dePaola

Directions:

Read *The Popcorn Book*. Discuss. How did the Native Americans pop corn? Where was popcorn first discovered? Have you ever eaten popcorn for breakfast with cream poured over it? Have you ever made popcorn by yourself? How did you do it? Ask the students to write about popcorn. They can describe how they make it, how the Native Americans made it, how and where they like to eat it, etc.

Popcorn Drawing

Materials:

popped popcorn, black construction paper, white chalk, white tempera paint, magnifying glasses (optional)

Directions:

Give each child a pile of popped popcorn. They may eat some, but save some to sketch. Ask them to examine the popcorn with the magnifying glass. If magnifying glasses are not available, they can examine the popcorn with the naked eye. Look carefully at all the ridges and parts of the popped kernel. Draw one big piece of the popped popcorn with their chalk on the black construction paper. Paint the drawing with white tempera paint.

Extension:

1. Does your popcorn look like a person, place, or thing? Can you name it? Can you write a story about this particular piece of popcorn?

2. Label your picture with a name and post it on the bulletin board.

3. Cut out all the popcorn pictures and place them popping out of a large paper skillet on the bulletin board.

4. Write captions for the popcorn. What would they say if they could talk to you?

5. Use popcorn to make pictures and label them.

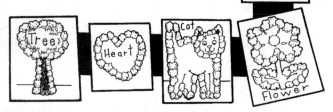

Best Ever Popcorn Activities (cont.)

Cooperative Popcorn Math

Materials:

popped popcorn, 9" x 11" black construction paper, white chalk

Directions:

Ask each child to find a partner or assign partners. Give each pair of children a handful of popcorn, one piece of black construction paper, and chalk. Spend a few minutes telling story problems such as the following. Let the children work the problems using the popcorn.

Five little popcorn men went popping out to say "Good Morning" to each other. One little popcorn man said "Good-bye" and left. How many little popcorn men are left?

Two little popcorn girls popped out to visit their friend. Suddenly one other friend popped out to surprise them. How many popcorn girls are there now?

Partner Story Problems

Ask the children to decide who will be the story teller first and who will solve the problem by moving the popcorn. When they have decided, let them begin making and solving story problems. In addition to solving the problem with popcorn, give the children paper and pencil and let them write the equations down. The story teller will check the work.

Extension:

Let the children decide which problem they want to save and write down the equation and paste on the popcorn to represent the problem. One or both children can write the story problem down and post it on the bulletin board beside the popcorn problem.

Fondue and Fruit Party

Silly Tilly had some fruit at her dinner. Which recipe contained fruit? We are going to learn more about fruit.

Materials:

1 jar marshmallow creme, 1 can chocolate frosting, fondue pot, sterno or candle, fruit, fondue forks or round at toothpicks, fruit, platter, paring knife, chart paper, 9" x 11" white paper, crayons, napkins

Teacher Preparations:

Make copies of the letter on page 29 and send home with children about one week before the fondue party.

Directions:

Ask the children to bring the fruit to the class in a paper bag. Have them give clues and let the children guess what fruit is in the bag. After they have guessed the name of the fruit, discuss each piece. Where a does it come from? Does it come in different colors? What does it taste like?

Record each fruit on the chart paper labeled

"Our Fondue and Fruit Party"

Kimberly brought an apple. It was _____ .
(Let the child write the color word describing the fruit.)

Brian brought an orange. It was _____ .

When all children have had an opportunity to write down the color of their fruit on the chart, have them a copy the sentence on the 9" x 11" paper. Have them illustrate their page with crayons. Make a class book out of these pages and let the children check it out overnight.

On the day of the party have the children peel and cut up the fruit. Make the Thanksgiving Fondue Dip. at Encourage children to taste all the fruit. Play the fruit card games on page 29.

Thanksgiving Fondue

Ingredients:

    1 jar marshmallow creme

    1 can chocolate frosting

Pour ingredients into a fondue pot and heat until melted. Children peel and cut up pieces of fruit for dipping. Use fondue forks or toothpicks for dipping the fruit in the chocolate.

Fondue and Fruit Party

Dear Parents,

Please send _____ to school on _____ . We are having a Fondue and Fruit party. Please come and join us.

Thank you.

Sincerely,

_____

These activities for Fruit and Vegetable Cards may be used with the fruit and vegetable cards found on pages 30 and 66. Color, cut, and laminate them or cover them with contact paper for durability. Play them at your Fondue and Fruit party.

1. Use the fruit and vegetable cards. Put them all in a bag. One child draws out a card and describes it to the class. They must guess which vegetable or fruit is being described from the clues being given.

2. Make two sets of fruit cards and play "Concentration" with them.

3. Write the names of the fruits and vegetables on the back of the cards. Use the cards as reading words and play a game with only the word side up. Match the cards and keep the pairs if you can read the words.

4. Mix the vegetable and fruit cards to make a more difficult "Concentration" game.

5. Use the vegetable and fruit cards together as flash cards and let the children tell you which is a vegetable and which is a fruit.

6. Use the cards as spelling words.

7. Give each child a card and let each use that fruit or vegetable in a sentence.

8. Write down the sentences the children have made up.

9. Place all the cards in a brown paper bag. Pass the bag around the circle. Let one child draw a card and tell the class what it is. The child keeps that card hidden from the other children. The next child must draw out another card and remember what the first person drew, plus tell the name of his/her fruit or vegetable (i.e. apple, pear).

Fruit Cards

Thanksgiving at the Tappletons'

by Eileen Spinelli

Summary

The Tappletons are having their customary Thanksgiving celebration. Their family is coming over to join them for turkey dinner with all the trimmings. Through a series of funny cooking mishaps the traditional dinner fails to appear. Grandma saves the day with a wonderful reminder of the true meaning of Thanksgiving.

Sample Plan

Day 1

- Show the cover of the book. Discuss families and who is in each child's family.
- Make a family portrait and label each person by name.
- Read *Thanksgiving at the Tappletons'*. Discuss what happened and why.
- Plan Grandparents' Day. (page 36) Write letters to grandparents. Send out questionnaires. Send letter home to parents.
- Begin to set up Ancestor Museum. (page 34)

Day 2

- Continue to set up Ancestor Museum. (page 34)
- Discuss Jenny and her problems with mashed potatoes.
- Teach the potato poem. (page 39)
- Draw potatoes. (page 41)
- Do potato dramatic play. (page 39)
- Copy the potato poem. (page 39)
- Play Potato Math. (page 40)

Day 3

- Work with Ancestor Museum. (page 34)
- Make Scarecrow Cornhusk Dolls. (page 59)
- Do some story telling with dolls. (page 60)
- Write books about dolls. (page 60)
- Make snacks for the Tappletons. (page 69)

Day 4

- Discuss immigration. (page 71)
- Invite a foreign speaker to class. (page 73)
- Write letters and make envelopes. (pages 73-75)
- Put up a foreign language bulletin board. (page 77)
- Do foreign language writing. (page 76)
- Start a foreign coin collection. (page 72)
- Graph coin collection. (page 72)
- Teach the Tappletons' song. (page 63)

Day 5

- Have Grandparents' Day. (page 36)
- Grandparent and child work on bulletin board. (page 77)
- With guests:
  –visit Ancestor Museum. (page 34) d
  –ecorate People Chains. (page 78)
  –make Acorn Necklaces. (page 61)
  –read Acorn Necklaces patterns.
  –play Native American Games. (page 70)
  –sing the Tappletons' Song.

Overview of Activities

Setting the Stage

1. Gather books about different countries and their people. Bring any items and clothing from foreign countries or from grandparents. Display these on a table or in a special area in the classroom.

2. Enlarge the map on page 79 and post it on a bulletin board. Label this bulletin board "Where Did Your Ancestors Come From?" Have yarn available for matching child's name or picture to the country of origin. On Grandparents' Day, the grandparents can help match up the countries with the students.

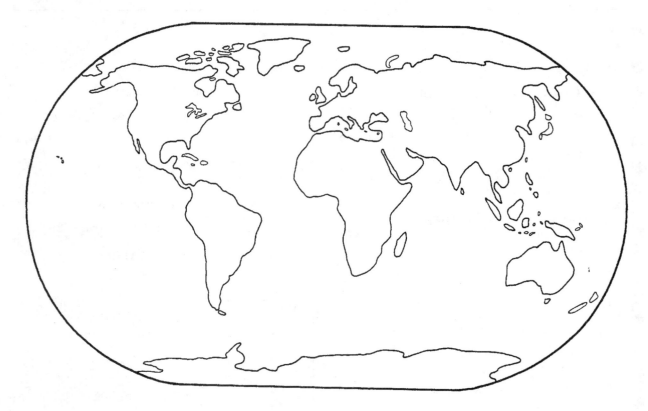

3. Write a caption for another bulletin board. "Can You Match the Grandparents and the Grandchild?" Post this on a bulletin board. When the children bring in their own pictures and those of their grandparents, post them separately on the bulletin board. The children can try to decide which child belongs with which grandparents.

4. Discuss families. If you have pictures available, show families of different ethic origins and groupings, i.e. single parent families, etc.

5. Have each child make a family portrait and label with the names of each person. Compile these in a class book. Make the book available for overnight check out.

6. Show the cover of *Thanksgiving at the Tappletons'*. Where are the grandparents, parents, aunts and uncles, and children? Does this look like your family? Compare the book cover to the children's family portraits

Overview of Activities *(cont.)*

Enjoying the Book

1. Read part of *Thanksgiving at the Tappletons'*. Stop reading after they discover there is no food. Ask the children what they think. What would they do if this happened to them at Thanksgiving? Each child can turn to the person on their left and tell them what they would do if they had no food at Thanksgiving.

2. Finish reading the book. Discuss what happened. What important thing did the family have?

3. Do some problem solving with the children. Ask them what Kenny could have done when he realized he had fed all the vegetables to the rabbits? What would they have done? If they had had the accident that Jenny did with the mashed potatoes, what would they have done?

4. Do some of the potato activities with the children. (See pages 39-41.) Teach the potato poem. Draw potatoes. Do potato dramatic play. Sing the potato song to demonstrate counting by 3's. Complete the potato math.

Extending the Activities

1. Plan Grandparents' Day. Write letters to grandparents and send out questionnaires. Let children know the they may "substitute" someone else for a grandparent if one is not available. Send the letter on page 38 home to parents.

2. Discuss the Ancestor Museum. Plan how to set it up and what each child will need to do to help with this project. (See page 34.)

3. Have a wonderful day with grandparents. The children and grandparents can cook (page 69), do joint art projects (page 58-61), take tours through the Ancestor Museum (page 34), get help from their grandparents in matching up pictures on the bulletin board, and sing the Tappletons' song on page 63.

Ancestor Museum

Discuss the word "ancestors." Talk about setting up an ancestor museum. Have children bring pictures of their ancestors and/or old items from their home. Set aside an area in your classroom where all these items can be displayed.

Materials:

index cards, marking pens, construction paper for signs, real pennies or paper pennies (page 35), plastic containers for pennies or cash register, baggies or small cups to hold pennies for museum customers

Teacher Preparation:

Make copies of pennies on page 35 for use with admission to the museum or use real pennies.

Directions:

Have the children make signs and label each item. Vote on a name for the museum and let teams of children make a name sign to display over the collection. When they bring something from home, they will need to explain to the class who the picture is or what the item was used for, or its origin.

Let the children choose a partner or assign partners and have one child tell their partner about their museum piece. That partner must explain that piece to the class or another set of partners. This requires good listening skills.

Variations:

1. Choose one child to be the curator and lead others through the museum.

2. Ask another class to visit your museum.

3. Charge admission to the museum. Let the children figure out change and handle all the transactions. Use a bag of real pennies or make paper pennies and let each child take a certain amount, which they must pay when they go in the museum. Place the pennies in baggies or small cups.

4. Make signs showing the price of admission.

   Adults .... $.05
   Children ... $.02

5. Make the math more difficult by changing the price. Let the children decide and change the prices and the signs. For instance, they might charge by color of clothing, or charge girls one amount and boys another amount.

If you are wearing		If you have	
red	$.02	brown eyes	$.03
yellow	$.03	blue eyes	$.02

This type of admission charging leads to all types of interesting discussions about fairness and prejudices.

Pennies for Ancestor Museum

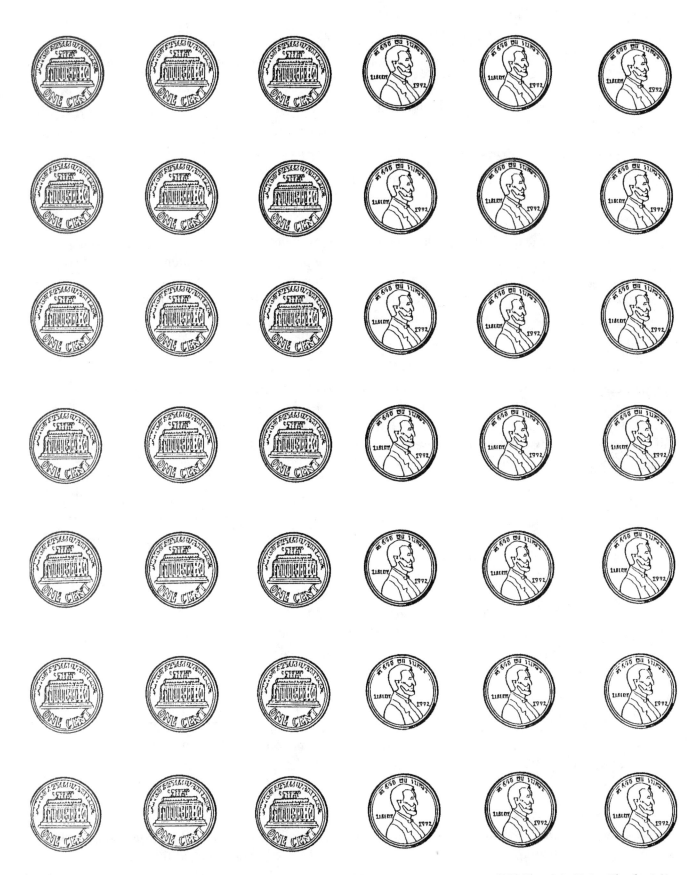

Grandparents' Day

Teacher Preparation:

1. About three weeks before Grandparents' Day, make copies of the questionnaire and the parent letter on pages 37 and 38. Send two or more copies of the questionnaire if the child has more than one set of grandparents. Send these letters home with each child.

2. Gather books on ancestors and grandparents for display in the library center in your room.

3. Put up the bulletin board with caption, "Can You Match the Grandchild and Grandparents?" This can be written on butcher paper, construction paper, or cut out with stencil letters.

4. Set up an area for the Ancestor Museum (page 34).

Materials:

Provide writing paper and pencils. Children may bring stamps and envelopes from home or you may furnish them. Another option would be to make the envelope on page 75. Children bring pictures of themselves and their relatives and food items for the cooking project. Children will need to have addresses of grandparents to copy on envelopes or send the letters home and ask the parents to mail them.

Directions:

Discuss with the class what they would like to do with their grandparents when they come to visit. They might suggest cooking with them, singing songs the class has learned, doing their regular work and having grandparents help, playing a game, doing an art project together, or a tour of the classroom and explanation of all that is happening. There are many activities throughout this book that would be great fun for children to share with a grandparent. After you have planned with the children, make lists of what will be needed and give everyone a job to do to get ready for Grandparents' Day.

Write a group letter to the grandparents asking them to tell about their history. This letter will accompany the questionnaire on page 37. The letter might look something like this:

```
Dear _____ ,

What country did you or your parents come from
originally? We are studying our history.

Love,

_____
```

The children can copy this letter or more mature students can compose their own letters. Address envelopes and mail letters.

Extension:

As the questionnaires come back from the grandparents, have the child read them to the class. Compile them into a "Grandparents' Book" and display it in the Ancestor Museum for all the look at.

Grandparents' Questionnaire

Please take a few minutes and answer these questions. We look forward to hearing your answers. Please return this questionnaire to your grandchild no later than _____ . THANK YOU!

Your Name _____ **Grandchild's Name** _____

- What country did your family come from?

  _____

- Did you have a big family? What was each member's name and relationship to you?

  _____

- What do you remember wearing to school when you were my age?

  _____

- Was there one outfit you really liked or really hated?

  _____

- Did you travel?

  _____

- Where did you go on your travels?

  _____

- What books did you read?

  _____

- Did you watch television?

  _____

- What work did you or do you do for a living?

  _____

- Where did your name come from?

  _____

- What did you eat for breakfast when you were a child?

  _____

- What was your favorite food when you were a child?

  _____

- Did you have a pet?

  _____

- Is there anything else you want to tell me about your life?

  _____

Invitation Letter

Dear Parents and Grandparents,

We are planning Grandparents' Day _____.
Please send a picture of your child and a separate picture of your child's grandparents if you have one. We want to put it on our bulletin board and see if we can match up grandparents and grandchildren. We also need the address of the grandparents so we can write class letters to invite them to our Grandparents' Day.

If your child does not have grandparents or the grandparents are unable to attend, please feel free to come spend the day with your child on Grandparents' Day. Or if your child has older people he/she would like to have attend in place of his/her grandparents, that would be wonderful too.

Do you have objects from the "olden days"? If you have items from your childhood or from your country of origin, we would like to put them in our ancestor museum for two weeks

We are planning a cooking project with the grandparents.
Please send _____ on or before _____.

Thank you for your help in making this a memorable time for your child and your child's grandparents.

Sincerely,

_____

Potato Activities

The Tappletons' didn't get any mashed potatoes for Thanksgiving. Unlike the Tappletons', let the children have some potato experiences.

Potato Poem

First recite the potato poem below. Then sing it using the tune "Ten Little Indians." When the song ends the children can either repeat it or add more numbers and continue the counting.

Potatoes

One little,

Two little,

Three little potatoes,

Four little,

Five little,

Six little potatoes,

Seven little,

Eight little,

Nine little potatoes,

Now let's add some more!

Potato Dramatic Play

Materials: copy of "Potatoes," the large potato the children drew in potato art (page 41)

Directions:

Ask for volunteers to pretend to be potatoes. Give each child a potato. One child will be potato number one, etc. As all the children sing the song, the nine potatoes come up to stand in groups of three, each holding a potato in front. Repeat the song until everyone has had a turn to be a potato.

Potato Poetry

Materials:

Potato poem enlarged or copied onto chart paper or the chalkboard, writing paper or journals, brown crayon, potatoes (optional)

Directions:

Have the students copy the poem in their journals or on writing paper. They may illustrate the poem with pictures of potatoes. Let each child find a partner or the teacher can assign partners. They can read the poem to each other and then practice reading it together. When they have practiced reading in unison, let them read the poem to the class. You might want to listen to the unison readings in several sessions, so students don't get bored listening to the same poem over and over again.

Variations:

Let the students practice reading it into a tape recorder. They love hearing themselves read. If you let students record their own reading often, you might want to provide a tape for each child. All student readings can be put on the same tape, but it becomes difficult to find individual student readings when they want to play it back.

Potato Activities *(cont.)*

Potato Math

Counting by 3's

Materials:

Nine potatoes or pictures of potatoes, copy of potato poem on page 39, number cards on page 18

Directions:

Use the potato poem to demonstrate counting by 3's. As you sing the song, group potatoes in groups of three or let the children do this as the song is sung. Have another child put the number cards by the potato groups.

Halves, Fourths, Eighths

Materials:

potato, knife, paper, pencil, brown crayon

Directions:

The teacher cuts the potato in half length wise or lets a student do the cutting. Discuss half and whole. Have each child draw a whole potato and a half potato on their paper and label "whole" and "half." Divide the potato in fourths and have the children draw and label the four parts on their papers. Do the same procedure with eights. What other Thanksgiving food could the children draw and divide in halves, fourths, and eighths?

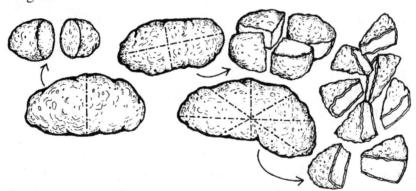

Potato Cooking

Materials:

potatoes, peeler or paring knife, pot of water, potato masher or fork, milk, butter

Preparation:

Peel potatoes. Place in a pot with water covering the potatoes. Bring to a boil. Let the potatoes boil until they are soft. Drain. Use the potato masher or a fork, add milk and butter to taste. (This can also be done in a blender, but watch so potatoes don't fly out!)

Potato Activities *(cont.)*

Potato Art

Materials:

drawing paper, oil crayons, pencils, different types of real potatoes

Directions:

Give each group of three children one potato and one set of oil crayons. Have them touch the potato. Ask the following questions: How does it feel? Is it rough or smooth? What color is it? What shape is your potato? Are all potatoes the same shape and color? After they have examined the potatoes, let them draw it. Caution them to make their drawings bigger than life size. Have them cut out their drawings and write their names on the back of the potato.

Extension:

1. Using green or brown butcher paper, make a potato patch and let the children place their potato in the patch or pile them all up in a big pyramid shaped pile in the garden.

2. Use these potatoes for counting by 3's on page 40.

3. Use potatoes with dramatic play on page 40.

Potato Print Wrapping Paper

Wrapping paper that children have made always adds a special touch to a gift. This is an excellent time to make some with potato prints using the potatoes you cut up to demonstrate ½, ¼, etc.

Materials:

raw potatoes (use the cut up pieces from potato math), knife, tempera paints, foam tray, large drawing paper or butcher paper

Directions:

Cut the potatoes in half. Carve a simple shape on the flat end of the potato. Triangles, stars, flowers, diamonds, rectangles, or a free form design will make nice prints. With the tip of the knife, cut an outline of the shape on the potato about ¼ inch deep. Use the knife to chip away all the other parts of the potato. Do not cut into the design. The design should protrude about ¼ inch above the surface of the potato. Put paint on a tray and dip the potato in the paint. Press the potato on the paper to make a print. The children might want to make rows or patterns using another shape. Or they may use a free form design and put the shapes in no particular order.

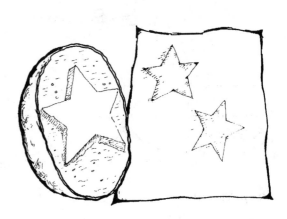

Turkey Feather Writing

Use the turkey picture on page 43 for the following activities:

1. Write a spelling word on each turkey feather.

2. Write an action word on each feather.

3. Write all names of the turkey body parts on the turkey.

4. Draw a picture or write a word that begins with "T" on each feather.

5. Write a short story on the body of the turkey.

6. Write the names of your classmates on the turkey feathers.

7. Write the things you are thankful for on each feather.

8. Write the names of all your family members on the feathers.

9. On the body of the turkey write what your family will do for Thanksgiving Day.

10. Write everything you know about turkeys on the body of the turkey.

Writing Thanksgiving Words

Materials:

paper, pencils, chalk, chalkboard, prizes such as stickers, or food treats for the winner or for all children who try to get many words, turkey (page 43)

Directions:

Number the papers to twenty. Copy the word "Thanksgiving" from the board. Try to make as many words as possible from this one word. The person with the most words gets a prize. As a variation, children may write the words on the turkey.

Turkey

Follow the Turkey Trail

Materials:

10 "T's" cut out from the pattern below, masking tape, a few feathers or a picture of a turkey in a box, a package of candy corn, copy of the letter on page 45

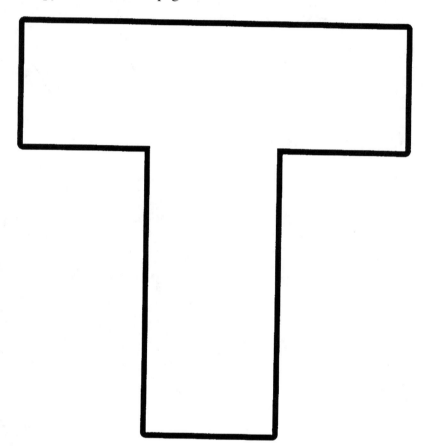

Teacher Preparation:

Make a trail for children to follow by taping "T's" around the classroom or school. Make arrows on the "T's" when you want the children to go in a certain direction or turn. At the end of the trail have a pile of feathers or a picture of a turkey in a box with a bag of candy corn. Copy the letter on page 45 and enclose the note in the box with the candy and feather.

Directions:

Organize the children into groups of 5 to 8. Caution them to remain silent about what they have found until all groups have had an opportunity to find the end of the "T" trial. When one group returns, send the next group. Instruct them not to bring the box back, but to just look inside and leave the contents and the box until all groups have had a chance to find it. The last group brings the box back to the classroom and it is opened with everyone watching.

While waiting for the groups to come back, play "The Turkey Hunt" on page 12 or discuss what the children will find. Will they find a real turkey? What do they think it will be? Write these ideas in their journals. Make a picture of what they think they will find at the end of the "T" trial.

Follow the Turkey Trail! *(cont.)*

Variations:

1. Have the children whisper "T-t-t-t" or make the "T" sound as they follow the "T" trail.

2. Each person in the group must think of a word that begins with "T" before going on the "T" trail or after they come back from the trail.

3. Change the letter and the contents of the box when you want the children to learn a different sound or letter

4. Write a word instead of a letter. i.e. turkey, dinner, etc., and let the children follow the word to the surprise.

Dear Class,

You're too late

Don't wait

I've gone through the gate

I'm not going to be handy

So eat this candy

It's ever so dandy!

Love,

Mrs. Turkey Lurkey

Turkey Put Together

Materials:

two sets of turkey parts on pelon, felt, or paper (page 47). (glue a piece of felt behind paper pieces), one large flannel board or two smaller ones

Directions:

Discuss turkey parts and show a picture of turkey. Use the turkey picture on page 43 or one from your own collection.

Game Directions:

1. Divide the class into two teams. This can be done by numbering off by 1's and 2's. As the children say their number, have them put that number of fingers up to remember which team they're on.

2. Give each player a turkey part. Each team should have enough parts to complete a turkey.

3. Have all the players on each team line up behind a starting line with their turkey part. (This can be drawn with chalk on the floor or rug.)

4. On the signal, "GO!" the first player in each line runs up and puts his/her turkey part on the flannel board, then runs back and touches the hand of the next team member. This continues until all members have had a turn and the turkey is complete. If the turkey is not put together correctly, the last member of each team needs to rearrange it so it will look like a turkey.

5. The first team to complete its turkey and have all players back in line is the winning team.

Variations:

Leave the turkey parts out in a center and let the children take turns putting it together with a partner or by themselves.

Write the name of the turkey part on the back of each piece. Let the child put it together on the table or floor using the back sides with words facing up.

Mix up the parts of the two turkeys between the two teams and see if they can cooperatively put the turkeys together.

Turkey Put Together *(cont.)*

Turkey Hand Math

Provide each child with one copy of this paper, crayons, pencil, candy corn, or counters. Have them draw around their left hand on the left side of the paper and the right hand on the right side of the paper. Color the thumb to look like a turkey head and the fingers to look like feathers. Make up problems such as: Feed the turkey on the left 2 pieces of corn. Take one piece away and give it to the turkey on the right. Continue with addition and subtraction facts. Emphasize left and right placement.

48

Corn Games

Estimating the Corn

Materials:

a glass or plastic jar, candy corn or real kernels of corn, large white piece of paper and marking pen or chalk and chalkboard, tens counting board (page 16)

Directions:

Ask the children to estimate how many corn kernels or pieces of candy corn are in the jar. Write down their estimations. Count the corn using the tens counting board. Compare the actual number to the children's original estimations. Which number was closest to the actual number?

Corn, Corn, Who Has the Corn ?

Materials:

one kernel of corn or candy corn

Directions:

Have all the students seated on the floor in a circle or have two circles of students and two games going at once. Each person clasps hands together but leaves a small opening between thumbs. One child is "It." There is one kernel of corn in "Its" clasped hands. "It" goes around the circle and pretends to drop the corn into the hands of each child. Into one of them the corn is actually dropped, but "It" continues around the circle until everyone is visited. All the children take turns guessing who has the corn. The person who guesses the correct student, gets to be "It" next.

Variations:

All the players sit in a circle and pass the corn from one to the other, being careful not to let the person who is "It" in the center see when they are passing. When "It" does see the corn being passed, the person passing it becomes the next "It.

Growing Sprouts for Turkey

Materials:

one empty quart jar, piece of cheesecloth or nylon net to cover opening of jar, rubber band, 2 T. alfalfa seeds or other types of edible seeds which will sprout, (available in a health food store or nursery)

Directions:

Drop the seeds in the jar. Put in 1 cup of water. Fasten the netting over the mouth with a rubber band. Shake the seeds and water gently together. Store in a dark place overnight.

The next day, pour off the water through the netting. Rinse the seeds daily with fresh water for the next week or so. Leave the jar in the light. Do not put the jar in direct sunlight, but near a window. After about a week, your seeds will be ready to eat. Put them in a turkey sandwich or in a salad.

Bean Pictures

Materials:

any dried bean or corn, 11" x 18" white construction paper, color crayons or oil crayons, glue

Directions:

Glue the bean on the bottom of the paper. Draw and color the plant that will come out of it. This may resemble the real plant or be an imaginary plant that has sprouted from the bean.

Extensions:

Write a story about this imaginary plant. What does it eat? Who lives in it? Where does it grow? Describe it in detail.

Planting Corn Seeds

Materials:
clean sponges or paper towels, baby food jars (one per child), different varieties of corn kernels, school milk cartons, soil, ruler, measuring cups or spoons (optional)

Teacher Preparation:
Collect, clean, and cut of the tops of small milk cartons. (Fifth and sixth graders love to help with this project!)

Directions:
Stuff the sponge or paper towel in the baby food jar. Pour in about ⅛ inch of water. The children can measure if you want to get in some lessons on measurement. Place the corn between the sponge or paper towel and the side of the baby food jar. Place the jar near light, but not in direct sunlight. Add water when the water level gets below ⅛ of an inch. The children will be able to see the changes in the corn kernel as it opens up and sprouts. In about 10 to 12 days the corn will sprout. Fill the milk cartons with soil. (This is best done outside.) Plant the corn sprout in the soil. Water the plants a little every day. Keep them in good lighting, but not direct sunlight. Take the plants home and when the weather gets warm, plant the corn outside. Water daily and watch your corn grow. (Corn needs lots of water.)

Extension:
What happened to the corn kernel? Sequence the pictures on page 52.

Sequencing Corn Planting

What happened to the corn kernel? Cut out the pictures and put them in the correct order.

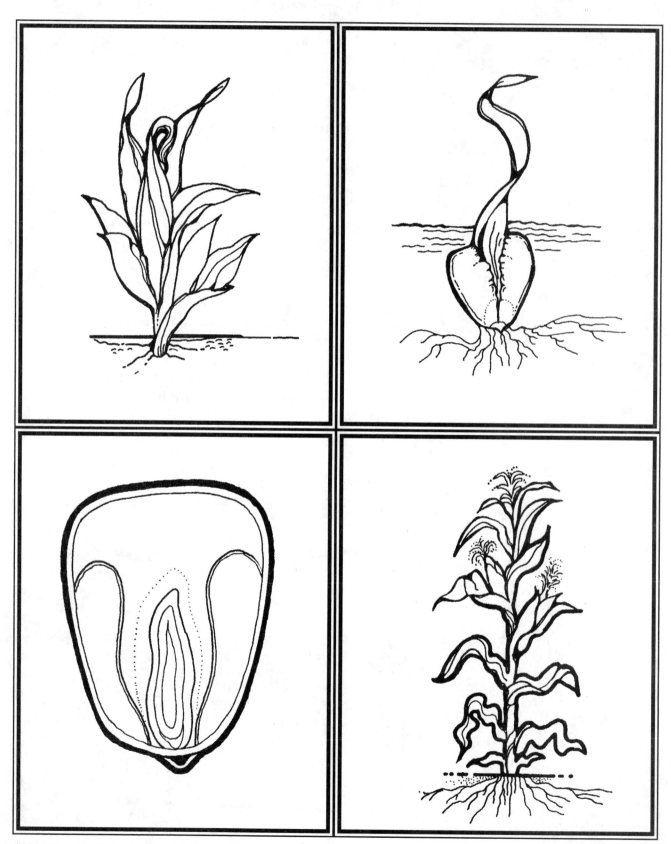

52

Feathers

Feathers have been used for many years in mattresses. Down is used in clothing, pillows, and quilts. Native Americans used feathers to decorate clothing and in ceremonial costumes. Wild turkeys have some very pretty feathers in their tails.

Read any of the following books: *Heather's Feathers*; *When Birds Change Their Feathers*; *My Feather*. Discuss birds and molting.

Take a walk and collect feathers. Have children bring them in to display in the science center. Display the different types of feathers and examine them with a microscope or a magnifying glass. Are the bones hollow or filled? Are all feathers shaped the same? Are they the same size, color, weight? Can you tell what bird the feather comes from?

Drop the Feather

Materials:
collection of feathers of different shapes and sizes

Directions:
Let a child stand on a chair or a table and drop each feather. Why do some feathers drop straight down and others spiral or drift down? Can you do anything to the feather to make it change its flight pattern? Do some feathers drop faster that others? Why? Does size or shape of the feather make a difference in the speed of the fall? Can you group the feathers by how they fall or by shape? (For example: rounded feathers versus straight feathers or fast fallers versus slow fallers.)

Science Experiment

Materials:
feathers, paper bags, fabric or plants, scales (optional)

Directions:
Fill a paper bag half full of feathers. Fill another bag half full of paper, fabric, or plants. Which bag weighs more? Which bag will drop the fastest?

Make a graph and let children predict what they think the outcome of the experiment will be. They can write their name under the column naming the bag that they think will drop the fastest.

Which bag will drop the fastest?	
Feathers	**Fabric**
Cindy Mlchael	Raylene

Drop the bags from a window or down a stair well. Which falls faster? Why? Now try this experiment with feathers in one bag and plastic blocks in another bag, or use some other heavier object. Which dropped the fastest? Why?

Feathers (cont.)

Feather Quill

Materials:

large feather, ink, paper, pictures of our ancestors signing proclamations with quill pens (optional)

Directions:

Dip the end of the feather in ink and try writing with it on the paper. Does it write well? Now use a pen. Which instrument writes better? Why?

Variations:

Tape a feather onto a pen and pretend it is a quill.

Draw a Feather

Materials:

drawing paper or construction paper, pens or pencils, feathers

Directions:

Give each child a feather. Let them examine it in detail and try to draw this detail into their pictures.

Feather Race

Materials:

two fluffy feathers

Directions:

Divide the class into two teams. Divide each team in half. Have the teams line up facing each other, with a space in between. The first player on each team must blow a feather across the room to the first player on his/her team on the other side of the room. (Distances no longer than 6 feet work best.) If the feather falls to the floor, the player must pick it up and continue blowing. The teammate must then blow the feather back across the room to another teammate.

When the last player on the team is done, the whole teams sits down. The first team with all members seated is the winner.

Variations:

The first team with no feathers dropped or the least number of feathers dropped is the winner.

54

Family Turkey Project

See page 8 for directions.

Dear Parents,

Today your child is bringing home a turkey. We would like you to decorate this turkey as a family project and return it no later than _____. All turkeys will receive an award and will be displayed on our bulletin board.

The turkey can be decorated in any way you would like. Be creative with anything you have around the house — seeds, fabric, paint, feathers, crayons, cotton balls, buttons, bows, noodles, cereal, etc. We hope your family will have fun working together on this project.

Sincerely,

_____

Family Turkey Project

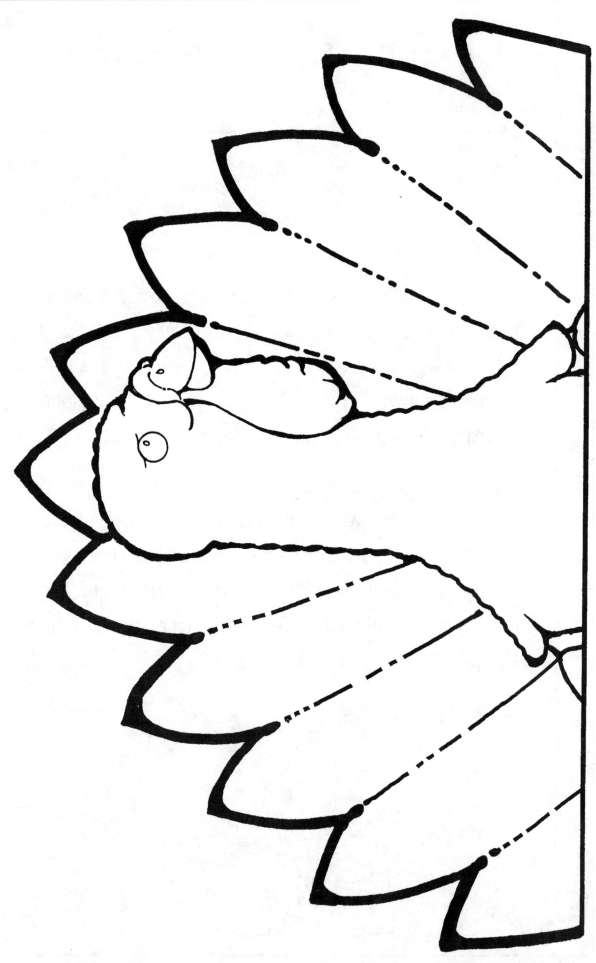

Paste tab under top of turkey

Turkey Headpiece

Materials:

One 1½" x 18" strip of white construction paper and one white strip cut 1" x 6" for each child; red, yellow, and various colors of construction paper; glue; scissors; stapler

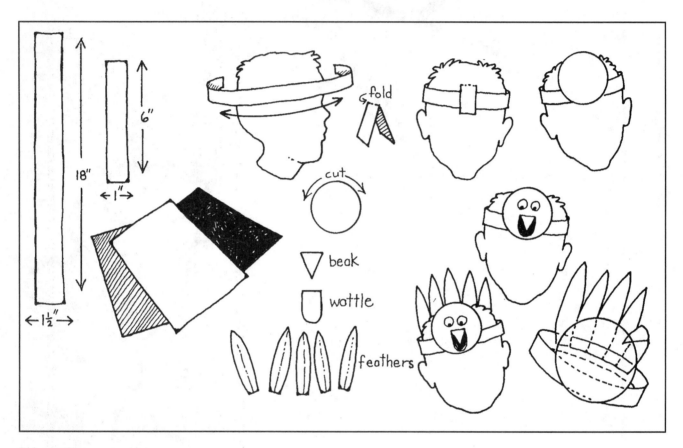

Directions:

Place the white strip of construction paper around the child's head and staple to fit. Fold the 1" x 6" paper in half and hang over the front of the headband. Have the child cut and glue a circle on this front strip for the turkey's head. Glue a yellow beak and a red wattle on the circle. Draw the eyes with crayons or paste eyes on the circle with black construction paper. Draw feathers out of various colors and paste or staple on the back of the headband.

Variations:

Have the children wear the headpiece and recite the following poem:

> **The Turkey**
> *I am a bird*
> *That goes wobble, wobble, wobble.*
> *I only know one word,*
> *And that's gobble, gobble, gobble.*

Scarecrow Cornhusk Dolls

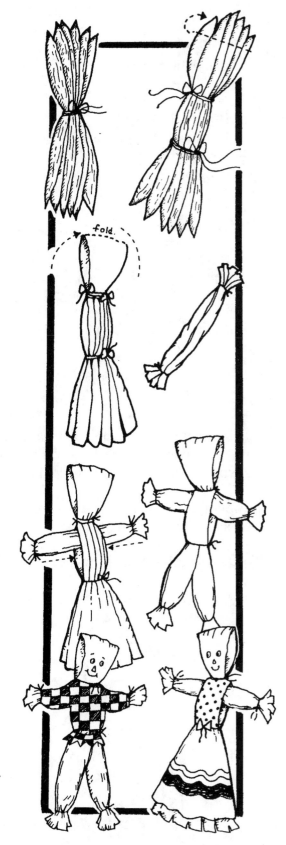

Teacher Information:

Cornhusk dolls were made by Native American children. These dolls are still made today and can be found in the Appalachian and Ozark Mountains entertaining children.

The husk is the foliage of the corn or maize plant that wraps the ear tightly in a protective coat. Cornhusks are tough. They can be braided, wrapped, twisted, and knotted.

Materials:

cornhusks (can be purchased in grocery stores in Mexican food sections), string or yellow yarn, water colors, scissors, paper towels, bucket or pan for soaking cornhusks, cloth or sponge, fabric, cotton (these last two items are optional)

Directions:

Soak the cornhusks in warm water until soft. This may take up to an hour. Drain them on paper towels. Keep the husks damp with a cloth or sponge while working with them.

1. Put 6 cornhusks together and tie a string around the middle for a waist. Tie another piece of string about 2" below the first for the body. Fold the ends of the husks down from the top and hold them down by tying them in place with another string placed on top of the first string that you tied in the middle.

2. Put two husks together and tie them near the ends with strings for arms and hands. Roll and slip the arms through the opening in the top of the body near the neck, or tie the arms to the body by wrapping string around them at the neck.

3. If you want a girl scarecrow, keep the bottom of the dress as is. To make a boy, divide or cut the husks below the waist. Roll into trouser legs and tie with string at the bottom of each foot.

4. Paint a shirt and skirt or pants to look like a scarecrow or a doll. Paint the features on the face also. Or, if you wish, use fabric and sew or glue clothes on your figure.

5. Add hair by gluing on paper strips, cotton, or fabric.

Cornhusk Doll Writing

After the children have made cornhusk dolls, they are ready to write a story about them.

Materials:

one small book for each student made of typing paper, construction paper, and staples, pencil, crayons

Teacher Preparation:

Make the small books by using standard typing paper. Cut it in half width-wise and fold it in half length-wise. This will make a book approximately 4" x 5". Cut construction paper covers and staple books together in the center.

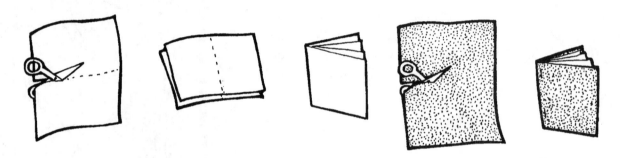

Directions:

Bring the children together in a circle with their cornhusk dolls. Let the children close their eyes and imagine that the doll is alive. What adventures would it have? Where would it live? What is its name? Have the children open their eyes and tell the person next to them about their doll. Let several children share their doll's story with the group.

Pass out the books and let the children write their doll's story in the book. They may use invented spelling or squiggle writing (scribble writing) if that is age-appropriate.

Illustrate their books with crayons.

Let them share their books with you and the class before they take them home.

Acorn or Button Necklaces

Teacher Information:

Native Americans used the acorn caps and buttons as jewelry and ornamentation on their clothing. Acorn caps can be found under oak trees in the fall. If you do not have them available, use wooden beads, buttons, or cereal.

Materials:

large needles (embroidery needles work well); heavy thread or plastic thread; acorn caps, round type cereal, wooden beads, buttons, or any other types of materials that could be used to make a necklace

Teacher Preparation:

You may need to thread and tie the needle so it does not continue to slip out as the child sews. Using a small nail or any sharp, pointed instrument, poke a hole in the center of each acorn cap.

Directions:

Before starting to sew, demonstrate the safe use of the needle. Have children sit apart when sewing, so they do not accidentally poke another child with the needle as they thread their necklaces.

Have the child lay all the materials out that they want to use in their necklace and make a pattern with it. Have them "read" their pattern to you before they start threading their necklaces. When the child has strung the necklace, tie the string together so the necklace will slip over the child's head easily.

Math Extension:

1. Have the children "read" the pattern on the necklace and convert it to numbers. For instance, an acorn, button, acorn, button pattern would be read as 1, 2, 1, 2 etc. An acorn, button, bead pattern would be read as 1, 2, 3, 1, 2, 3, etc.

2. Have the children count the total number of items on their necklaces.

3. Count the number of acorns only, buttons only, and add up the total. Which item has the most on the necklace?

4. Count the items by 2's, by 5's, and by 10's.

Thanksgiving Songs

Sing these songs after reading the stories or while working on Thanksgiving projects.

Use with *Silly Tilly's Thanksgiving Dinner*

"Here We Go Over To Silly Tilly's"
Sing to the tune of "Here We Go Round the Mulberry Bush"

Here we go over to Silly Tilly's,
Silly Tilly's, Silly Tilly's,
Here we go over to Silly Tilly's,
On Thanksgiving Day.
Mrs. Squirrel brought acorn jam,
Acorn jam, acorn jam,
Mrs. Squirrel brought acorn jam,
On Thanksgiving Day.
Mr. Woodchuck brought nut cake,
Brought nut cake, brought nut cake,
Mr. Woodchuck brought nut cake,
On Thanksgiving Day.
Mr. Chipmunk brought cranberry stew,
Cranberry stew, cranberry stew,
Mr. Chipmunk brought cranberry stew,
On Thanksgiving Day.
Mrs. Fieldmouse brought oat bran pudding,
Oat bran pudding, oat bran pudding,
Mrs. Fieldmouse brought oat bran pudding,
On Thanksgiving Day.
Mr. Bunny brought potato pie,
Potato pie, potato pie,
Mr. Bunny brought potato pie,
On Thanksgiving Day.
Mr. Turkey brought corn to pop,
Corn to pop, corn to pop,
Mr. Turkey brought corn to pop,
On Thanksgiving Day.
It was the very best Thanksgiving,
Best Thanksgiving, best Thanksgiving
It was the very best Thanksgiving
The animals had ever had!

62

Thanksgiving Songs *(cont.)*

Use with *Silly Tilly's Thanksgiving Dinner.*

"Silly Tilly Forgot"

Sing to the tune of "Old MacDonald Had a Farm"

Silly Tilly had a dinner
E-I-E-I-O
And, at her dinner, she forgot to cook
E-I-E-I-O
With "Oh dear, " here and "Oh dear, " there
Here, "Oh dear," there "Oh dear"
Everywhere "Oh dear"
Silly Tilly had a dinner
E-I-E-I-O

Use with *A Turkey for Thanksgiving*

"Hickory, Dickory, Lurkey"

Sing to the tune of "Hickory, Dickory, Dock"

Hickory, Dickory, Lurkey
Mr. Moose ran up to the turkey
The turkey hid away
Mr. Moose had his say
And turkey went home anyway.

Use this song with *Thanksgiving at the Tappletons'*

Set the poem at the end of the Tappletons' to music.
Tune: "Hush Little Baby Don't Say a Word"

Turkeys come and turkeys go
And trimmings can be lost, we know.
But we're together and
That's what matters
Not what's served upon the platters

Turkey Soup

Materials:

hot plate and large kettle or large electric skillet, broth, bowls, spoons, paring knife, vegetable peeler, hot pads, ladle, large spoon, chart paper or butcher paper, marking pen, copies of letter below

Teacher Preparation:

1. About one week before the feast, send home the letter below.

2. The night before the feast, simmer 2 turkey legs in about 3 quarts of water. Cool, remove meat from bone and cut in small pieces. Take the broth and cooked turkey to school on the day of the feast. (This can be made ahead and frozen.) Or buy large cans of chicken broth and canned chicken.

Directions:

As each child brings in their vegetable to add to the pot, write it down on a chart entitled "Turkey Soup."

Turkey Soup
We made turkey soup.
Marita brought potatoes
August brought carrots.
Karl brought tomatoes.
Erik brought onions.

If the vegetables need peeling or cutting, let the children prepare them. Cook the vegetables in the broth until tender.

Send home this letter a week before the soup-making or let the children dictate a letter and write it on the board for all to copy.

Dear Parents,

We are making turkey soup on _____ . Please send _____ with your child on or before that day. We will add it to our soup.

Thank you.

Sincerely,

_____

Turkey Soup *(cont.)*

Turkey Soup Math

Materials:

chart used from soup making or the actual vegetables, pen, individual chalkboards and chalk or paper and pencil, crayons

Directions:

If you have the actual vegetables, give one to each child or let them hold the one they brought. Count all the vegetables and record that number on the chart or the chalkboard. Place the vegetables in sets of 2 and count by 2's. Continue the same procedure for counting by 5's and counting by groups of 10 Having the children place the vegetables in groups of 5 and 10 gives them practice in grouping. When the vegetables are in groups of 5, have one child take away one vegetable. How many are left? Have the children record this equation on their chalkboard or paper. Continue playing this game with sets of 5, 4, etc. Continue the same procedure with sets of 10.

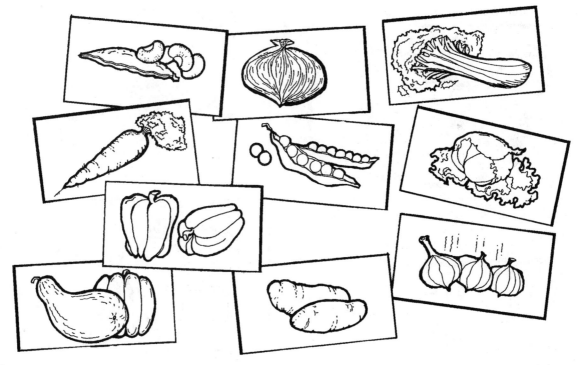

Variations:

1. Use a set of number cards 0-10 and plus and minus symbol. See page 18. Have the children practice making equations with the vegetables and then placing the number cards beside the vegetable to show the equation.

2. If you can't use the vegetables, use the cards on page 66, or use any counters you have in the classroom.

3. Read *Stone Soup* to the class and count all the vegetables used in that soup. Did they use the same vegetables in *Stone Soup* as we used in our soup? What was different?

Vegetable Cards

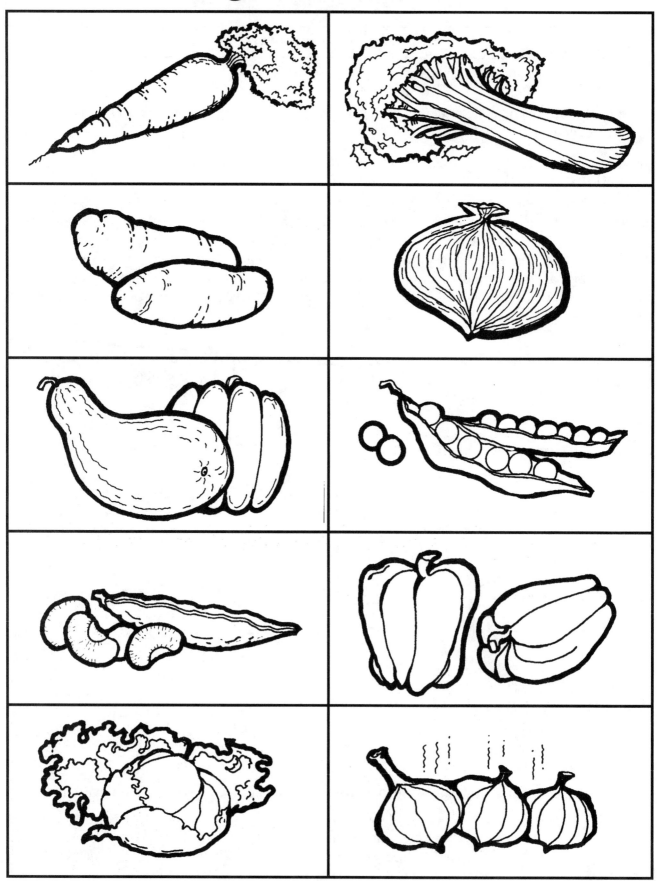

66

History of the Cranberry

Pilgrims found a small, sour, red berry, which they called "cranberry" because its drooping, arched blossoms reminded them of the long neck and head of the crane, a well-known bird in Europe. The word cranberry comes from a partial translation of Low German, "Kraanbere."

Native Americans used the cranberry juice to dye rugs and blankets and also to heal wounds. They made poultices from unripe cranberries. They believed that the cranberry had the power to calm nerves and remove poisons.

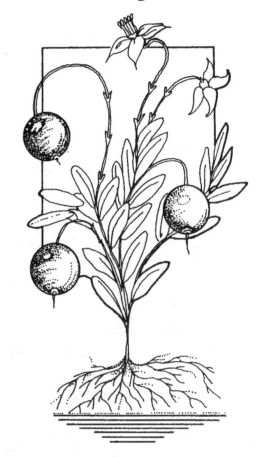

Wild cranberries ripened and were eaten fresh or ground, or mashed with cornmeal and baked into bread. They were also dried for use in the winter. To sweeten the berries, they were mixed with honey, maple sugar, or syrup. They were used in making pemmican, too. One version of pemmican used mashed cranberries, smoked deer meat, fat, and wild onions boiled together. This was pounded into cakes and allowed to dry in the sun. These pemmican cakes were used on trips. Word of the delicious berries spread to England and were in demand there. In 1677 New Englanders sent ten barrels of Massachusetts cranberries, packed in spring water, to King Charles II of England as a gift. Cranberries kept many months without spoiling when packed in water.

Cranberries grow in fields known as "bogs." They need a base of acid soil or peat, fresh water, and sand. They also require a long growing season without severe frosts. The ocean climate of Cape Cod, Southern New Jersey, Wisconsin, and the Pacific Northwest are ideal for this berry. The cranberry is one of the three fruits which are native to North America. The blueberry and the Concord grape are the other two.

Cranberries are often eaten at Thanksgiving time. Mr. Chipmunk brought Cranberry Stew to Silly Tilly's dinner. This recipe (page 68) as a relish will simulate that dish.

Thanksgiving Recipes

Mr. Chipmunk's Cranberry Stew Relish

Materials:

baby food jars with lids, grinder, knife, bowl, large spoon, small spoon, colander

Ingredients:

2 lb. cranberries, 8 oranges, sugar to taste

Have groups of 4-5 children work together. Rinse cranberries in the colander. Put cranberries in grinder and grind up. (Children love to do this.) Peel oranges and grind up. Mix ground oranges with ground cranberries. Add sugar until it tastes sweet enough. Let the children sample and decide when the relish has enough sugar. Each child may spoon cranberry mixture into a baby food jar to take home.

Extension:

1. Let each child copy the recipe and take it home with the cranberry relish.
2. Write a group story about how the children made the relish.
3. Dramatize the Native Americans using cranberries to heal wounds. Have one child be the medicine man and another the patient.
4. Discuss other fruits that taste sour, such as lemons and grapefruit.

Writing and Recipes

Silly Tilly's Recipes

Materials:

5" x 7" or larger note-cards, pencils, crayons

Directions:

Make recipes for Mr. Woodchuck's Pine Nut Cake. This could be done as a group activity and written on the chalkboard. The children can copy the recipe on the note-cards, or each child can write their own recipe for Pine Nut Cake on the note-cards. Do the same activity with Mr. Chipmunk's Cranberry Stew, Mrs. Fieldmouse's Oat Bran Pudding, and Mr. Bunny's Sweet Potato Pie.

Variations:

1. Have the children illustrate a picture of their food item to post beside or glue on back of the recipe card.
2. Let them write their own original recipe that they would take to Silly Tilly's Thanksgiving dinner.
3. Make a class recipe book of original recipes. (These can be totally ridiculous recipes or serious attempts at cooking.)

Snacks for the Tappletons

Apple Snow

Materials: mixing bowl, electric beater, mixing spoon, hand graters, plastic spoons and cups or bowls

Ingredients: 2 cups grated apple, 1½ cups powdered sugar, 4 egg whites

Let the children take turns peeling and then grating the apples. Show them how to separate egg whites from egg yolks. Beat the egg whites until stiff. Slowly add sugar and beat. Fold in grated apple. Serve on small plates or in small cups. This recipe will make enough for each child to have a small serving.

Stuffed Dates

Materials: pitted dates, shelled walnuts, granulated sugar, small bowls, knife

Directions: Stuff a pitted date with a shelled walnut. Place sugar in small bowl and roll the date in it. Eat and enjoy!

Stuffed Celery Tree Trunks

Materials: paring and table knives, mixing bowl, mixing spoon, measuring spoon, ruler

Ingredients: celery, 1 tsp. mayonnaise, 3 oz. cream cheese, a few drops of worcestershire sauce, paprika

Have the children measure and cut the celery into 4" pieces. Leave some of the stalks with celery leaves at the top to resemble tree leaves. Mix together all the ingredients except celery. Stir until it is creamy and easy to spread. If needed, add more mayonnaise. Spread filling in celery stalks. Press two stalks together. Stand them upright to resemble tree trunks.

Native American Games

Blindfold Game

Teacher Information:

Native Americans hunted for their food. They had to learn to be very quiet when sneaking up on a deer. They also had to learn to listen very well so they could hear animals in the woods.

Materials:

blindfold (piece of fabric or dish towel), large feather or piece of fake fur, or a piece of fabric

Directions:

One child is blindfolded in the center of the circle, holding a feather or whatever object is being used. Other children are seated in a circle around the blindfolded child. One child is chosen to sneak up quietly and try to touch the blindfolded person before being hit by the feather. If the child is hit, he/she returns to the circle and another child gets a turn. If a child is not hit, he/she becomes the next blindfolded player. Take turns until all have had a turn to be either a blindfolded person or a "sneaker."

Variations:

Divide the class into groups of 10 players in a circle and have several games going on at once.

Bowl Game

Materials:

24 almonds, walnuts, or peanuts in their shells, marker, 4 small plastic bowls or containers, box of toothpicks

Directions:

Draw a thick line on one side only of each nut. Divide the class into small groups around five different bowls. Put six nuts in each bowl. One person holds the bowl, flips the nuts in the air and tries to catch them again in the bowl. Each player gets one point for each nut that lands with the marked side up. For every point, the player takes one toothpick. Each player gets three turns. The player with the most toothpicks at the end of the three turns is the winner.

Variation:

Change the rules. If the nuts land with the unmarked side up, the player gets a point. Vary the number of turns and the number of nuts in the bowl. Instead of using toothpicks, teach the children how to use a tally sheet and keep track of their own score with tally marks.

70

Immigration of People

Teacher Information:

Many immigrants have come to North America over the years. Immigrants from all over the world still continue to come. When we look at all the cultures we have here today, we can appreciate the diversity and richness that this allows all of us to experience.

Discuss the origin of Thanksgiving and the fact that our ancestors came from many different countries. Thanksgiving is a time for saying, "Thank You." to this great country we live in.

Social Studies and Geography

Materials:

large map of world or enlarge page 79, string or yarn, push pins or tacks, paper to make labels for map, photographs or names of children

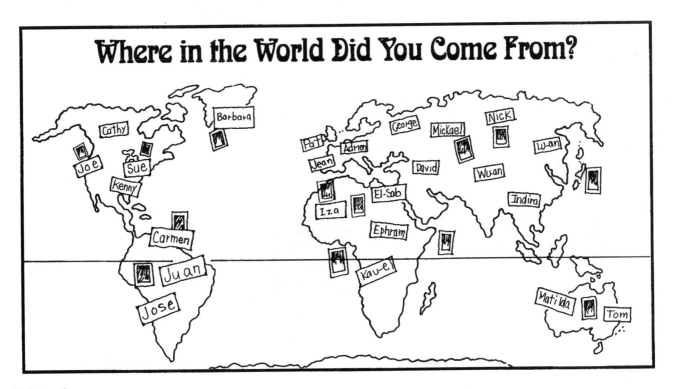

Directions:

Ask children to find where their families originally came from. Laminate a map of the world and let children put string lines from their country of origin to their home. They can place their name or their picture on the yarn line. Older children can label countries on a blank map and then put yarn up to show their country of origin.

Variation:

On Grandparents' Day, have the grandparents help match up the yarn.

Foreign Coin Collection

Converting to Dollars

Materials:

table or space for collections, paper or note cards for labels, marker or pens

Directions:

Start a foreign coin collection by asking children to bring in coins from foreign countries. Have them label each coin with the name of the country it came from. Older children can look up exchange rates in the newspaper and convert to dollars and label the coins with that information. Make a graph showing the different coins and what they are worth in dollars.

Variations:

Compare coins in terms of size, shape, color. Provide egg cartons for storing coins by size, shape, color, and/or worth. Or make another graph showing size from largest to smallest.

Letter Writing

Materials:
writing paper, chalk, chalkboard

Teacher Preparation:
Locate a person from another country who would be willing to visit your classroom and talk to the children about his/her home country. Get the person's name and address and arrange a time for him or her to come.

Directions:
Have the children compose a group letter to invite this person from another county into the classroom. As the children dictate the letter, write it on the board for the children to copy.

Dear _____ ,

We would like to hear about your country. Could you come to our class and tell us about your way of life? We would like to learn to say "Thank you," "Please," "Hello," and "Good-bye," in your native language. Please come on _____ , _____
                                                          Day   *Date*
at _____ .
      Time

Sincerely,

_____

Let the children help decide which child's letter should be mailed to invite the speaker. Or send all the letters to the speaker. See page 74-75 for ideas on making and addressing the envelope.

Variations:
1. To help students with grammar, spelling, punctuation, etc., let them pass their letter to the person beside them for checking or turn in the papers to you to get help in correcting the errors.

2. Recopy the letters and send to the speaker.

Addressing Envelopes

Materials:

envelope pattern on page 75, glue or tape, scissors, pencil or pen, legal size envelope, stamps (optional)

Directions:

Cut out the envelope on the solid lines. Fold on the dotted lines to make an envelope. Tape or glue the bottom flaps together.

Demonstrate on the chalkboard how to address a letter. Explain each line and the placement of it on the envelope as you address the envelope. Have the children address their own envelopes to the speaker, if they are sending individual letters. If not, have them address the envelope to themselves.

If they address it to themselves, this will give them practice learning their own addresses and zip codes, as well as learning the mechanics of addressing letters.

Speaker in the Classroom

Before the speaker arrives, have the children help make a list of possible questions to ask. When the person comes to the classroom, provide a time for the children to ask questions. Let the person answer in his/her own language for a few minutes to give children an opportunity to hear the rhythm of that language. Have them guess what they think the answers to the questions were. Have the person teach the children to say simple phrases in the language. i.e. thank you, please, hello, etc. Write these phrases down and post them in your room. Children can copy them later and take them home to teach to their families. Have the class write a thank you note to the visitor using some of the foreign phrases in the note.

Envelope Pattern

1. Cut on solid lines.

2. Fold bottom up on broken line.

3. Fold side flaps over and glue in place.

4. Fold top flap down and seal after inserting letter.

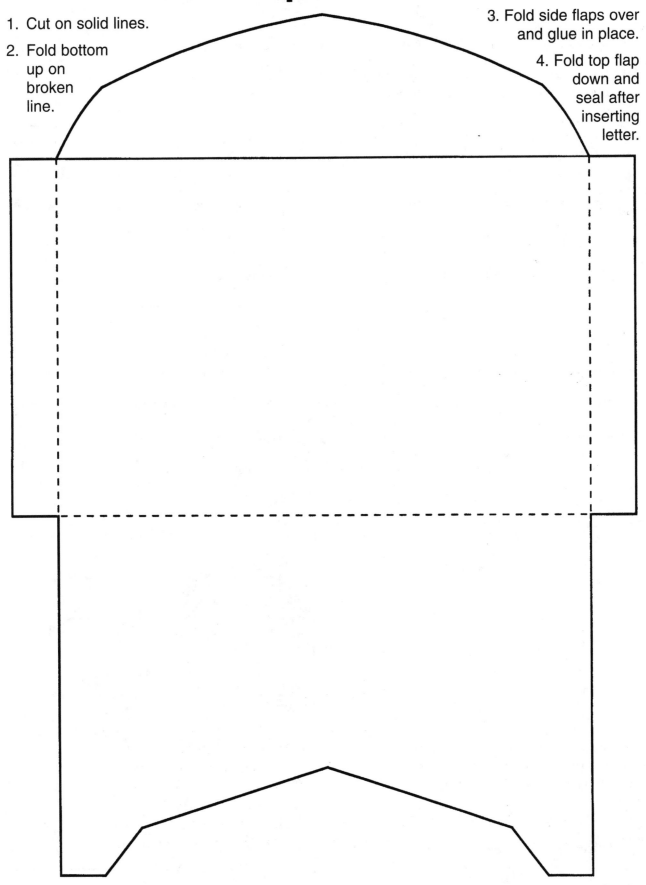

Language Study

"Thanks" in Foreign Languages

Have the children research all the ways to say "Thanks" in different foreign languages. Post these on a bulletin board with the world map. (page 79)

Arabic: sohoukran	Latvian: paldies	Polish: dziekuje	Swedish: tack

Here's a list of how to say "thanks" in several languages.

Arabic:	*shoukran*	Portuguese:	*obrigado*
Czech:	*dehuji*	Rumanian:	*multumiri*
Danish:	*tak*	Russian:	*spasîbo*
Dutch:	*dank*	Serbo-Croatian:	*hvala*
Esperanto:	*dankon*	Spanish:	*gracias*
Estonian:	*dekui*	Swahili:	*asante*
Finnish:	*kiitos*	Swedish:	*tack*
French:	*merci*	Turkish:	*tesekkür*
German:	*danke*	Yiddish:	*dank*
Greek:	*efcharisto*		
Hebrew:	*todah*		
Hungarian:	*koszonom*		
Indonesian:	*terima kasih*		
Italian:	*grazie*		
Japanese:	*arigato*		
Latvian:	*paldies*		
Lithuanian:	*tanan*		
Norwegian:	*takk*		
Polish:	*dziekuje*		

"Thanks" Bulletin Board

Use the "Thanks" bulletin board for writing ideas.

1. Let each child chose a country and copy that country's word for "Thanks." Have them write a
   sentence using that word.
   Mother says "_____" when I take out the trash.
   Or, Jacob loaned me his scissors and I said, "_____, Jacob."

2. Pretend you are a child going to school in a foreign country and the only word you know in that
   language is "Thanks." How would you ask for a pencil? How would you ask directions to the
   lunch room?

People Chains

How do you think these people in foreign countries dress? What do they look like? Do they look like
you?

Materials:

white butcher paper 16" x 48" (you will need one of these strips for every four children in your class),
crayons, colored chalk or paints, scissors, tagboard fabric scraps, buttons, ribbon, etc.

Teacher preparation:

Tear off and cut butcher paper into 16" x 48" strips. (If you want to make larger or smaller people, vary
the size of the strips.) Enlarge the pattern on page 78 to fit on the strips. Make one or more patterns out
of tagboard for the children to copy. For younger children, trace the pattern on the strips and let the
children cut them out.

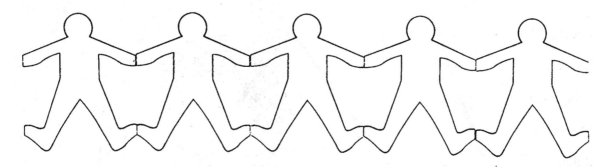

Directions:

Organize the children in groups of four. Show them how to fold the butcher paper to make chains of
people. (Fold the butcher paper in half width wise and then in half again and in half again.) Trace the
pattern on the folded butcher paper. Make sure the middle of the body, as well as the ends of the arms
and legs, are touching the folds. Do not cut these folds. Cut the person through all layers of butcher
paper. Unfold. Count the number of people. How many people did you make? Working in groups of
four or with grandparents, each child will decorate a person from the country they are studying. They
may use fabric scraps, buttons, crayons, etc. When everyone is finished, tape them together in a long
line and hang them up for display.

People Chain Pattern

World Map

Bibliography

Fiction Core Books

Bunting, Eve. *A Turkey For Thanksgiving.* Clarion Books, 1991

Hoban, Lillian. *Silly Tilly's Thanksgiving Dinner.* Harper & Row, 1990

Spinelli, Eileen. *Thanksgiving at the Tappletons'.* Harper & Row, 1982

Fiction

Asch, Frank. *Popcorn.* Parent's Magazine Press, 1979

Baker, Betty. *The Turkey Girl.* Macmillan, 1983

Balian, Lorna. *Sometimes It's Turkey, Sometimes It's Feathers.* Abingdon, 1973

Carter, Anne. *Molly in Danger.* Crown Publishers, 1987

Child, Lydia. *Over the River and Through the Wood.* Coward, McCann & Geoghegan, 1974

Cohen, Miriam. *Don't Eat Too Much Turkey!* Greenwillow, 1987

dePaola,Tomie. *The Popcorn Book.* Holiday,1978

Dragonwagon, Crescent. *Alligator Arrived with Apples.* Macmillan, 1987

Glovac, Linda. *The Little Witch's Thanksgiving.* Prentice-Hall, 1976

Hallinan, P.K. *I'm Thankful Each Day!* Ideals Children's Books, 1981

Janice. *Little Bear's Thanksgiving.* Lothrop, Lee Shepard, 1967

Johnston, Tony. *Happy Birthday Mole and Troll.* G.P. Putnam, 1979

Livingston, Myra Cohn. *Thanksgiving Poems.* Holiday House, 1985

Miller, Edna. *Mousekin's Thanksgiving.* Prentice-Hall, 1985

Moncure, Jane Belk. *My First Thanksgiving Book.* Children's Press, 1984

Pilkey, Dav. *'Twas the Night Before Thanksgiving.* Orchard Books, 1990

Prelutsky, Jack. *It's Thanksgiving.* Greenwillow Books, 1982

Ross, Dave. *Tiny Turtle's Thanksgiving.* William Morrow, 1986

Schatell, Brian. *Sam's No Dummy, Farmer Goff.* J.B. Lippincott, 1984

Stock, Catherine. *Thanksgiving Treat.* Bradbury, 1990

Weiss, Leatie. *Heather's Feathers.* Avon Camelot, 1976

Wickstrom, Sylvie. *Turkey on the Loose!* Dial Books, 1990

Williams, Barbara. *Chester Chipmunk's Thanksgiving.* Dutton, 1978

Wood, Audrey. *The Horrible Holidays.* Dial, 1988

Nonfiction

Barth, Edna. *Turkeys, Pilgrims, And Indian Corn.* Clarion, 1975

Cauley, Lorinda Bryan. *Things to Make and Do for Thanksgiving.* Franklin Watts, 1977

DeLage, Ida. *Pilgrim Children on the Mayflower.* Garrard, 1980

Fritz, Jean. *Who's that Stepping on Plymouth Rock?* Coward, McCann & Geoghegan, 1975

Gans, Roma. *When Birds Change Their Feathers.* Thomas Crowell, 1980

Gemming, Elizabeth. *The Cranberry Book.* Coward-McCann, 1983

Gibbons, Gail. *Thanksgiving Day.* Holiday House,1983

Jupo, Frank. *The Thanksgiving Book.* Dodd, Meady & Company, 1980

Mainwaring, Jane. *My Feather.* Doubleday, 1989

Patent Hinshaw, Dorothy. *Wild Turkey, Tame Turkey.* Clarion Books, 1989

Weisgard, Leonard. *The Plymouth Thanksgiving.* Doubleday, 1967

Wyndham, Lee. *A Holiday Book, Thanksgiving.* Garrard,1963.